Smoking 101

An Overview for Teens

Smoking 101

An Overview for Teens

Margaret O. Hyde

John F. Setaro, M.D.

TFCB Twenty-First Century Books
Minneapolis

Cover photograph courtesy of © SuperStock

Photographs courtesy of © Michael Newman/PhotoEdit: p. 10; © The Granger
Collection, New York: p. 61; © Reuters Picture Archive: p. 63; © Mark
Dadswell/Getty Images: p. 69; The BADvertising Institute, http://www.
badvertising.org, © 1986 Bonnie Vierthaler: p. 71

Data source for the diagrams on pages 24, 35, 51, 55, 81, and 86 is
The Tobacco Atlas by Dr. Judith Mackay & Dr. Michael Eriksen.
Used by permission of the World Health Organization.

Twenty-First Century Books
A division of Lerner Publishing Group, Inc.
241 First Avenue North
Minneapolis, Minnesota 55401 U.S.A.

www.lernerbooks.com

Library of Congress Cataloging-in-Publication Data
Hyde, Margaret O. (Margaret Oldroyd)
Smoking 101 : an overview for teens / by Margaret O. Hyde and John F. Setaro.
p. cm.
Includes bibliographical references and index.
ISBN-13: 978-0-7613-2835-3 (lib. bdg. : alk. paper)
ISBN-10: 0-7613-2835-1 (lib. bdg. : alk. paper)
1. Tobacco—Toxicology. 2. Smoking—Health aspects. 3. Teenagers—Tobacco use.
I. Setaro, John F. II. Title.

RA1242.T6H98 2006   616.86'5—dc22   2004022757

Manufactured in the United States of America
3 4 5 6 7 8 – BP – 12 11 10 09 08 07

Contents

The First Cigarette Won't Kill Me

Just about everyone old enough to read this book recognizes the fact that smoking is risky. While smoking rates for teens are at a historic low, 4,400 young people between the ages of twelve and seventeen in the United States start smoking every day, 2,000 of whom will become daily smokers[1]. They all know the first cigarette won't kill them.

What's all the fuss about smoking? Many preteens and teens believe that it is safe to smoke a pack of cigarettes a day and then quit in a few years. Some figure that there will be a cure for cancer by the time they might need it. Many decide they will make the choice to smoke and stop when they feel like it.

The truth is that if you begin to smoke, you will be one of three kinds of tobacco users. One group becomes *addicted* quickly. A second group of people, the largest group, gets hooked gradually, after a period of regular smoking. Others can smoke lightly and drop the habit easily because they are not addicted. The problem, unfortunately, is that you can't tell in advance what will happen to you when you begin to smoke.

How Long Does It Take to Get Hooked?

In the past, almost everyone thought that one had to smoke for a long time to become dependent on *nicotine*, the drug in tobacco that keeps people smoking. In 2002, Dr. Joseph R. DiFranza of the University of Massachusetts at Worcester and some of his colleagues reported the results of a study they did over a period of thirty months.[2] They learned that the first symptoms of nicotine dependence can appear within a matter of days after the first cigarette. They found that young people can lose control over the choice of whether or not they want to smoke after twenty or fewer cigarettes. In some cases, a kid's fate was sealed with the first cigarette.

Scientists have recently learned that teen brains are a work in progress, and changes in the structure of their brains make teens more vulnerable to becoming addicted. Therefore, the teen years are a time when tobacco companies hope you will begin smoking their brand of cigarette or start using their brand of *snuff* or *spit tobacco*. They need you to replace the adults who have quit and those who have died.

The First Cigarette Is a Kid Thing

If you reach the age of twenty without smoking your first cigarette, you will probably never smoke. In other words, just about no one starts to smoke after reaching the age of twenty. It seems to be easier for younger people to make the choice because they very likely don't have all the facts.

Lifetime smoking almost always begins before high school, or the age of fourteen. Do you know someone who started smoking at ten years of age? Some kids begin at eight or even younger. About one tenth of smokers tried their first cigarette at the age of ten or before, and about 80 to 90 percent of adult smokers started smoking before they were eighteen years old.[3] The average age for the first cigarette is thirteen. The majority of kids who begin smoking before or in their teen years are daily smokers by the time they are eighteen years old. Those who begin to smoke at a younger age are more likely to develop long-term smoking habits than late starters. The rates of nicotine dependence are greater for young smokers than for any other age group.[4]

Then Why Do Some Kids Start?

Reasons for choosing to smoke the first cigarette differ. Many kids begin out of curiosity. They want to know how it feels to smoke, to find out what is

In the United States, the average age for smoking a first cigarette is thirteen.

so great about smoking that so many people are doing it.

Peer pressure is one of the most common reasons for trying a first cigarette.[5] Although not many parents encourage their kids to smoke, sisters and brothers who smoke often do.

According to researchers, concern about body image and weight control is responsible for more smoking at an earlier age than previously thought. In one study, about 20 percent of the girls who started smoking were preoccupied with attractiveness, and 30 percent of the boys were worried about being overweight. But this study also showed that smoking does not always help to make a better body image.[6]

Children who live in families where there is psychological, physical, or sexual abuse of them or their parents; substance abuse; or other criminal behavior are more likely to start smoking earlier and smoke more than those who live in healthier situations. These children tend to have low self-esteem and be more susceptible to peer pressure and ads for cigarettes. They tend to use smoking as a coping mechanism.[7]

Researchers at the University of Pennsylvania and Virginia Commonwealth University have found an association between the first cigarette and variations in a *gene* related to a system in the brain that is involved in mood and behavior. If you inherit this gene from both parents you are likely to begin smoking at an earlier age than if you did not.[8]

And, last but far from least, kids are strongly influenced by the subtle messages of tobacco advertising. Kids want to feel like adults. They think smoking will make them look more grown up and sophisticated like the people in the ads. Girls somehow think that smoking would make them seem sexy and desirable, while boys want to seem masculine and cool like the rugged men in ads for cigarettes. They buy into the images attached to the ads by the big tobacco companies. Tobacco companies spend billions of dollars a year to advertise their products. They tell you their cigarettes are cool, make you more attractive, help you have more fun, and make you look more mature. They make it look as if all attractive people smoke their kind of cigarette. Are they messing with your mind? If you believe the ads then they probably are. The best way around that is to make your own decisions based on the truth.

The Good News

Year after year it has been much the same. New smokers, mostly young people, take the place of those who quit and those who died, but the numbers are different now. Recently, there have been some important changes in how teens view smoking. Today, many teens are saying tobacco use is dangerous, cigarettes cost too much, and their friends would disapprove of their smoking. Many of them feel that smoking is no longer socially acceptable. Some of those who can't stop even try to hide their cigarettes from both friends and parents.

> **As of December, 2003, 22.9% of high school students and 10.17% of middle school students in the United States were current cigarette smokers.**

According to a recent report by the University of Michigan and the National Institute of Drug Abuse, an increasing number of young people say they see smoking as dangerous, more say they disapprove of smoking and *smokeless tobacco* use, and more say their friends would not approve of their smoking.[9]

In spite of the ads that show smoking as glamorous, sexy, and attractive, the proportion of students saying that they prefer to date nonsmokers rose from 64 percent in 1997 to 72 percent in 2002, but remained at 72 percent through the next two years. With nearly three-quarters of the opposite sex saying that they prefer to date people who do not smoke, it is clear that young people pay a social price for becoming smokers.[10] University of Michigan studies, Monitoring the Future, have been tracking the smoking habits of high school seniors each year since 1975. Grades 8 and 10 were added in 1991 and have been surveyed annually along with high school seniors.[11]

It is not only social prohibition that is cutting the number of teen smokers. Smoking is banned in more places than ever before, so finding a place to smoke can be very inconvenient. Restaurants used to have smoking sections, but most eating places are totally nonsmoking now. People can no longer smoke in offices, in public buildings, on public transportation, or even in many bars.

In January 2003, when New York City passed a ban on smoking in nearly all of the city's bars and restaurants, a tough ban on indoor smoking was already in place. When the new law passed easily, one reporter noted that only the very young and very stupid consider smoking a sophisticated thing to do.[12]

Another deterrent is that smoking can be an expensive habit, especially for the teens who spend a large part of their allowances buying cigarettes. Some street kids get their nicotine by picking up discarded cigarette butts, but with higher taxation on cigarettes, these butts are becoming shorter. It's also harder to bum a cigarette, a practice commonly used by many smokers who are trying to quit. Actually, increasing the cost of cigarettes is considered a major factor in smoking prevention.

With less social acceptance of smoking, fewer places to smoke, more information about health risks, and the higher price of cigarettes, the rate of smoking among middle school and high school students declined sharply in the first two years of this century. Teen use of cigarettes has been dropping steadily since the peak rates in 1996 and 1997. Between 2001 and 2002, the proportion of teens saying they had ever smoked cigarettes fell more than in any recent year.[13] The number of American teens who were current smokers in 2004 was down from peak levels in the mid-1990s by one half for the nation's 8th and 10th graders and by one third among its 12th graders.[14] In recent years, teen smoking has continued to decline, but the declines are slowing. [15]

Most young smokers still believe that the number of smokers is greater than it really is. Many think it is twice as common as it really is. Apparently misery craves company!

Nicotine: The Addiction Culprit

Some smokers enjoy the feel, the smell, and the sight of a cigarette and the ritual of handling and lighting a cigarette, cigar, or pipe. Some people feel that smoking makes them sophisticated and worldly. Others are lured by cigarette advertisements. But whatever reason people have for smoking cigarettes, cigars, or pipes, or enjoying smokeless tobacco, such as snuff or chewing tobacco, they are reacting to nicotine. Without nicotine, they would probably give up smoking.

Anatomy of a Cigarette

A cigarette looks simple: just a paper wrapped around some tobacco, but today's cigarette is a very carefully engineered nicotine delivery system. You can read the amount of nicotine and tar a brand contains on its package. These amounts are carefully controlled as tobacco companies vie for the lowest amount of tar. (Tar is everything but the nicotine and water.)

The paper that wraps the tobacco is a very special kind of paper. It plays a major part in how fast the cigarette burns—slowing it when the tobacco is not being inhaled, and speeding the burn rate when the smoker is taking a puff from the cigarette. Did you ever wonder why a lighted cigarette that is parked on an ashtray doesn't go out? There are chemicals in the paper that keep the cigarette burning and control it when the smoker takes a drag so that the smoke is delivered evenly.

Only part of the inside of the cigarette comes from untreated leaves of the tobacco plant. If you dissected a cigarette, you would find three kinds of tobacco in many of the most popular brands. There are some untreated leaves, and there are tobacco stems and inferior parts of the leaf that have been made into a mash. This mash is sprayed with hundreds of chemicals and sliced to resemble tobacco leaves. Another part of the cigarette is puffed tobacco, which is made of freeze-dried leaves that have been treated to increase the volume.

In 1954, when the public became aware of the connection between cigarettes and lung cancer, tobacco companies began offering various kinds of filters on their cigarettes to help lower the tar content and other toxins in the smoke. Some companies added charcoal to the dense, synthetic material of which the filter is made but there is no evidence that this makes cigarettes significantly less dangerous.[1] Small holes in the filter tip allow air into the smoke. This makes the cigarettes test lower for tar and nicotine when smoked by a tobacco company's machine, but smokers often cover these holes with their lips or fingers. Cigarette smoking machines record lower rates of tar and nicotine than the rates produced by a human smoking the same cigarette.

Tobacco companies would like you to think that *"light" cigarettes* are safe to smoke. The ads may say "low tar, low nicotine," but these cigarettes are not necessarily less harmful. They may increase the health risks from tar and other harmful products in smoke because many smokers of so-called safer cigarettes compensate by smoking more and/or inhaling more deeply.[2]

A Nicotine Delivery System

Since nicotine is the drug that makes smoking pleasurable and is the part that causes *addiction*, it is the reason a smoker has cravings for the next cigarette. About an hour after smoking a cigarette, the smoker feels irritable until he or she smokes again. Just a few puffs on a cigarette make life better. No wonder it is hard to quit.

A typical smoker inhales about ten puffs on a cigarette in the five minutes or so that the cigarette is lit.[3] An average smoker inhales about 300 times a day, unconsciously adjusting the nicotine level to one that makes him or her comfortable. Nicotine is in a smoker's blood all day, the level rising as each cigarette is smoked. The level declines until the next hit. Although the level drops during the night, there is still some nicotine present in the morning.

The first cigarette of the day rescues the smoker who is addicted to nicotine from *withdrawal* symptoms. That cigarette is the one many smokers say they enjoy most. When measuring how much a person is addicted to nicotine, one of the questions is, "How long are you awake before you smoke your first cigarette?"

A cigarette has been defined as a highly efficient device for getting nicotine to the brain. More than 90 percent of what is inhaled is absorbed by the lungs,[4] where nicotine rides into the body on tiny particles of tar. The nicotine is quickly absorbed into the blood, and it reaches the brain about ten seconds after the smoker inhales. This is faster than if it were injected with a hypodermic needle, the way *heroin* is put into the body. By the end of fifteen seconds, nicotine reaches the big toe, the farthest outpost of the body.

Nicotine goes from the tiny branches of the lungs into the blood, where it picks up oxygen. From there it is carried in the blood to the heart and pumped around the body. Nerve cells in the brain are affected by nicotine the same way that they are affected by *cocaine* and *amphetamines*. The nerve cells in the body communicate with each other through chemicals called *neurotransmitters* that travel in the tiny spaces between the cells. The chemicals fit into receptors on the surface of the nerve cells that are receiving them.

Nicotine is shaped like one of the neurotransmitters known as *acetylcholine*. This chemical and its receptors are involved in many functions, including muscle movement, breathing, heart rate, learning, and memory. When nicotine gets into the brain, it mimics the action of acetylcholine and attaches itself to the acetylcholine receptors, so stimulating effects are exaggerated at first. The nicotine remains in these receptors and blocks out acetylcholine, thereby limiting its activity and producing a calming effect. So nicotine first stimulates, then it calms.[5] It also causes the release of other neurotransmitters and hormones that affect such things as appetite, mood, and memory. One major effect of smoking is the increased level of a kind of neurotransmitter called *dopamine* that is part of the brain's reward system. All addictive drugs increase the amount of dopamine and produce pleasure and reward.[6] These pleasurable effects cause the smoker to seek them again. And since this stimulation is followed by depression, the person seeks more nicotine. As use continues, changes take place in the brain that act to increase the number of times a person uses tobacco. When this continues, the user becomes addicted.

Nicotine does more than make a person feel good. It increases alertness, intellectual skill, and concentration; enhances memory; and improves problem-solving ability. It also reduces appetite, decreases tension, and relaxes skeletal muscles.[7]

As mentioned earlier, addiction to nicotine can happen with some people within days or weeks of smoking only occasionally. Others who smoke may not become addicted for months or even years. You may know people who can stop smoking whenever they feel like it. They may smoke several cigarettes a day and do not become addicted. Most beginning smokers figure this is what will happen to them. They think they will smoke a few cigarettes now and then, but will never have a craving for cigarettes. This kind of thinking is called optimistic bias. It is the tendency to assume that risks apply only to other people. Unfortunately, only a small percentage of new smokers don't become addicted.

What Is Addiction?

For many years, nicotine was not recognized as an addictive substance, but today there is no question about it. To fit the definition of addictive, there must be symptoms of withdrawal when the drug is stopped. Withdrawal from nicotine is well recognized. The urge to smoke, irritability, difficulty concentrating, and feelings of anxiety or restlessness are some withdrawal symptoms. An addict may suffer from all or just some of them. A second characteristic of addiction is *tolerance* to the drug. Tolerance to nicotine develops quite rapidly, even more quickly than it does to heroin or cocaine. Addicted smokers gradually increase the number of cigarettes they smoke from a few cigarettes a week to a few a day, and then often to one or more packs a day. The rate of addiction is similar for twins who are identical, and thus have the same genes. This suggests that nicotine tolerance and dependence runs in families.[8] A third criterion for addiction is the importance to the user. Most smokers don't resort to deviant behavior, but that is because they have easy access to nicotine. Many smokers admit doing things

Nicotine addiction is the most common drug addiction in the United States.

they would not normally do if they did not need a cigarette so badly, smoking used butts from an ashtray, for example, when cigarettes are not available.

War prisoners who were given very limited amounts of food have gone hungry after exchanging food for cigarettes. In undeveloped countries, parents with starving children have been known to barter food for cigarettes. You may know someone who hates the cold but goes outside several times a day in mid-winter to satisfy his or her *craving* for cigarettes.

Another characteristic of addiction is continuing use even in the face of harmful circumstances. Almost everyone knows something about the health risks of smoking and other forms of tobacco use. About 35 million people try to quit each year, but only a small percentage actually succeed.[9]

Nicotine may not be the only substance in cigarettes that is addictive. Scientists are able to watch changes in the brain using imaging known as *magnetic resonance imaging* (MRI) and they have seen that smoking causes a marked decrease of a substance known as *monoamine oxidase* (MAO), an important enzyme that is responsible for breaking down dopamine. This results in higher levels of dopamine and may be another reason that smokers continue to smoke: to sustain high dopamine levels, which leads to the desire for repeated drug use.[10]

Some brain changes during withdrawal from tobacco addiction are similar to those that occur during the withdrawal from other abused drugs.[11] Rates of dependence (the percentage of users who experience symptoms that reinforce their drug use and have trouble quitting) are higher for nicotine than for *marijuana*, cocaine, or alcohol.[12]

A Dirty Delivery System

Suppose you are watching television and you suddenly see a message: "Traces of *cyanide*, *mercury*, *acetone*, and *ammonia* have been discovered in a widely consumed commercial product." When this message was shown on French television, about a million viewers called the toll-free number given on the screen to get more information. Those who were able to complete the call discovered the answer: cigarettes.[13]

Smokers smoke for the effect of nicotine, but they get a lot more. Manufacturers add chemicals to make cigarettes taste and smell better. Some of these—such as chocolate, caffeine, and yeast—are safe as foods, but they change when heated and burned. Cigarettes are a dirty delivery system, with more than 4,000 compounds present in the smoke that is inhaled to produce a pleasurable feeling.

As mentioned earlier, many chemicals are added to tobacco when cigarettes are made. One of these, ammonia, is added to cigarette tobacco to release more nicotine. Among the toxic chemicals that form when a cigarette burns are tar particles that make up the visible part of the smoke. The lungs of a person who smokes a pack or more of cigarettes a day is exposed to a total of one and one-half pounds of gooey black tar a year.[14]

Deadly Chemicals

Tobacco smoke includes	as found in
Acetone	paint stripper
Ammonia	floor cleaner
Arsenic	ant poison
Butan	lighter fluid
Cadmium	car batteries
Carbon Monoxide	car exhaust fumes
DDT	insecticide
Hydrogen Cyanide	gas chambers
Methanol	rocket fuel
Naphthalene	moth balls
Toluene	industrial solvent
Vinyl Chloride	plastics

Tobacco smoke contains more than 4,000 chemicals, some 60 of which are known or suspected to be carcinogens.

The invisible part of the cigarette smoke contains many toxic gases, including *carbon monoxide, hydrogen cyanide,* and *formaldehyde.* Fertilizers used by farmers to grow tobacco plants add heavy metals that stay in the tobacco and are part of the smoke that is inhaled. Chemicals called *nitrosamines* are particularly bad carcinogens (cancer-forming chemicals). The government regulates the amount of nitrosamines permitted in the bacon we eat, but it does not protect smokers from nitrosamines that they inhale when they smoke.

I'll Get My Tobacco Elsewhere

A **common** misimpression among young people is that it is the cigarette that is unhealthy, so if they can get their nicotine from other sources, the danger is lessened. Not so!

Cigars

With the concern about cigarettes and health, many people turn to cigars, thinking they might be a safe alternative. Cigars are defined as a compact roll of tobacco leaves prepared for smoking. Today, cigar tobacco leaves are aged for about a year and then fermented in a process that can take three to five months. This causes changes in the tobacco that give cigars a different taste and smell from the tobacco in cigarettes. Cigars come in many different varieties.

Cigars first became popular in the early 1800s. Although cigarettes are still much more common than cigars, cigars have gained in popularity in recent years. Tobacco companies have changed the image of cigars by showing cigar smoking as stylish and as a symbol of wealth and power. Cigars have been glamorized by movie stars and athletes, making them popular with men and women and making them a status symbol to some young people. According to two wide studies conducted in California, cigar use has increased nearly five times among women and appears to be increasing among adolescent females as well. Furthermore, a number of studies have reported high rates of use among preteens. Cigar use among older males (age sixty-five and older) has continued to decline since 1992.[1] Cigar bars and lounges, where smoking and alcohol consumption give people a place to smoke, drink, and enjoy each others' company, are often considered upscale.

Smokers are wrong in thinking that cigars are a good alternative to cigarettes. Many smokers think cigars are safer because they don't inhale the smoke. Actually, typical cigars have seven times more tobacco than cigarettes, and tars from tobacco can cause oral cancer. The nicotine content of some cigars is as great as that of a whole pack of cigarettes. Premium cigars are smoked for about ninety minutes, while about two cigarettes are smoked in an hour. No matter how they are smoked, cigars still put people at risk for health problems.

Smokeless Tobacco

As with cigar smoking, many people consider smoke-less tobacco (snuff or chewing tobacco) safer than cigarettes. Snuff is powdered tobacco that is usually sold in cans. It is put between the lower lip and the gum where it is quickly absorbed by the bloodstream. The nicotine acts on the brain, giving pleasure while the chemicals in the tobacco affect the gums.

Chewing tobacco is usually sold as leaf tobacco, packed in a pouch, or as plug tobacco, sold in brick form. Both are put between the cheek and gum and kept in the mouth for a short time.

The use of moist snuff and other types of smokeless tobacco in the United States almost tripled from 1972 to 1991. Now more than 2,200 young people try spit tobacco and 830 become regular users every day. That means 304,000 new spit tobacco users each year.[2] It has been estimated that 3 million people under the age of twenty-one years use spit tobacco regularly.

Every time smokeless tobacco is used, the body adjusts to the amount needed to get the same feeling. Gradually, users need more nicotine to get the same results; they have developed a tolerance for nicotine. When chewers and dippers build tolerance, they turn to smokeless tobacco with more nicotine in it. Like cigarette smokers, they are addicted, and this addiction makes it hard to quit.

Gutka

Many children in India and other countries are addicted to *gutka*, a form of smokeless tobacco made from a mix of lime paste, areca nut, spices, and tobacco sealed in plastic or foil. Smoking is taboo for most children and teens, but gutka is socially acceptable for many children, especially in India. It is as convenient as chewing gum and as sweet as candy, but it is responsible for an alarming increase of oral cancers in children in India. India has 75,000 to 80,000 new cases of oral cancer a year, most of which come from smokeless tobacco.[3] Some states in India banned the production, transport, and possession of gutka.

Are Bidis Safe?

Bidis (pronouced beedies) are small, flavored cigarettes tied with colorful threads at each end. They are extremely popular in India and among some teens in the United States. Bidis are smaller than popular brand-name filtered cigarettes, and are hand-rolled in tendu leaf instead of the kind of paper used for American cigarettes. Tendu is a broad-leafed plant native to India; its leaves are not porous like the paper wrap of a traditional cigarette. This means less air can mix with the tobacco as it is smoked, so the smoke is more concentrated. A smoker has to draw hard to keep a bidi lit. In India, bidis have no added flavor, but in the United States, they are flavored with chocolate, vanilla, strawberry, licorice,

In the United States, an estimated 2.6% of high school students and 2.4% of middle school students are bidi users.

mango, root beer, or grape, making them especially appealing to middle-schoolers. Many kids who smoke bidis have no idea about what they contain. They have a street reputation as "natural" products, leading many young people to consider them safer than cigarettes.[4]

Kreteks

Kreteks are *clove cigarettes* that are smoked by about 90 percent of Indonesians who smoke.[5] They have also been popular in parts of China and other countries for many years. Now, they are gaining in popularity in some other countries, including the United States. They contain a blend of tobacco and cloves as well as other flavors from herb extracts and fruits. Kreteks come wrapped in white, brown, and black paper, and may be smoked as an alternative to regular cigarettes by people who continue to smoke both. They are not safer than regular cigarettes.

Hookahs

Using a *hookah* to blow smoke has become popular in some cafés, especially those found near colleges and universities in sections where many Yemeni, Moroccans, Egyptians, and other Arab immigrants live. A hookah is an ancient Middle Eastern water pipe that uses sweetened tobacco. A user takes a puff and passes the hookah to a friend, who takes a puff and passes it on. This is usually done in a Middle Eastern setting where friends enjoy hanging out with something they think is harmless.

Tobacco suppliers claim that because the scented tobacco used in hookahs is grown in soil with low nitrogen, the nicotine is lower than in common cigarettes. It is still possible to develop an addiction from it, according to Danny McGoldrick, research director for the Campaign for Tobacco-Free Kids. Many of the cafés that offer hookahs serve coffee and tea, so they are considered restaurants and come under the Smoke-Free Air Act, which prohibits smoking in restaurants in many cities. So, along with other kinds of blowing smoke, this ancient custom is being restricted by modern laws, too.

Nicotine Without Tobacco?

As antismoking laws increase and smokers find they must huddle in doorways to get their nicotine, John Leland, a *New York Times* writer, dreams of satisfying cravings for nicotine by eating food that contains it. There is nicotine in many common foods, such as tomatoes, potatoes, and red peppers, but, according to Jack Henningfield, who is an expert on addiction, you would have to eat a hundred pounds of tomatoes to get a dose that would replace the nicotine you crave.[6] What about adding nicotine to coffee? Any recipe that contained enough nicotine to satisfy a smoker would poison him or her.

After the smoking ban that stopped smoking in New York City bars in 2003, some restaurants actually did offer "Tobacco Specials" on their menus. You could order a steak filet with tobacco-wine sauce, a tobacco-infused grappa, or a smokeless Manhattan cocktail that tasted like tobacco. One restaurant owner claimed that food with tobacco tasted better than smoking. However, there were questions about whether or not one could really taste the very small amount of tobacco that was safe in food or drinks. The tobacco menus were a novelty, but they didn't supply enough nicotine to stop the craving.

So it's back to blowing smoke outdoors in any kind of weather or quitting.

Candy Cigarettes

Do you remember smoking candy cigarettes? They are not as popular with children as they used to be but they are still being produced. They come packaged in boxes that are labeled with names that mimic adult brands of cigarettes. Some are a chocolate variety with cellophane wrappers, some are the traditional white with red tip, and others are bubble gum with brown tips and sugar inside that can be blown out in particles that look somewhat like smoke. Several studies have shown that children who use imitation cigarettes are twice as likely to smoke tobacco as those who don't.[7]

Candy cigarettes have been suggested as a humorous gift for a friend you hope will quit smoking real cigarettes. They may be the only safe way to blow smoke.

Chapter 4

My Smoking and My Body: The Physiology of Smoking

Everyone who smokes knows that after the first few cigarettes, smoking can be very pleasant. Who would continue to smoke if there were not some enjoyable aspects to it? Obviously, nicotine addiction is the primary reason people who don't want to be smoking continue doing it—but there are other people who don't want to stop. They can find a lot of positive things about smoking.

Smoking is a highly sensual experience. Most smokers have a ritual that involves their sense of touch. They tear the pack open neatly, extract the first cigarette, tap it on the nearest flat surface or the back of one hand, and insert it between their lips. Then they light the cigarette and deeply draw in the first smoke. This feels great to them. The sense of sight is involved as they look at the cigarette that will bring them further pleasure. They watch the smoke as it wafts through the air. The familiar taste of tobacco and the odor of the cigarette make them feel good, too. Even people who are trying to quit smoking are tempted to smoke when they smell someone else's freshly lighted cigarette.

Most smokers know that nicotine reaches the brain on the fast track, where it produces pleasurable sensations.[1] Each puff produces a spike of immediate satisfaction. A smoker can hold the smoke in the lungs, or take deeper or more frequent puffs to increase pleasure. If the smoker increases the nicotine level to an overdose, he or she feels dizzy or nauseated and cuts back on the dose.

As mentioned earlier, tobacco use improves mood, decreases tension, and relaxes muscles, and for a short time, it improves attention, learning, reaction time, and problem solving. This sounds great. Why all this fuss about smoking prevention? That's a stupid question that almost anyone can answer. There are all those diseases that happen when you get old, but most young people feel, "They won't happen to me."

What Smoking Can Do While You Are a Teen

Within one minute of starting to smoke, your heart rate begins to rise. It may increase by as much of 30 percent during the first ten minutes of smoking and it does not return to normal until after smoking has stopped.[2] When another cigarette is smoked, the heart rate increases again. Smoking raises blood pressure. About 20 minutes after you stop smoking, your blood pressure drops back to a level close to what it was before the last cigarette. Just a single cigarette can lower temperature in the hands and feet. Nicotine causes narrowing of the small blood vessels, depriving the tissues of some of the normal supply of oxygen.

The carbon monoxide in smoke deprives tissues of the body of some of their normal supply of oxygen.[3] It takes eight hours after smoking for the carbon monoxide level in the blood to drop to normal. Carbon monoxide from smoking lowers the amount of oxygen available to the body because it combines with some of the *hemoglobin* in the blood, making less oxygen available for cells all over the body. Smoking hurts physical fitness in terms of both performance and endurance even among people trained in competitive running.[4] It can slow down reaction time, and increase shortness of breath. Smokers suffer shortness of breath almost three times more often than nonsmokers. And there is less oxygen available to the muscles during physical activity.

Tobacco affects the body in many ways. It can cause irritating symptoms such as stinging eyes or stained teeth or dull senses of taste and smell. But tobacco is the cause of much more serious, often fatal, diseases such as various types of cancer, particularly lung cancer, as well as heart disease, strokes, and emphysema.

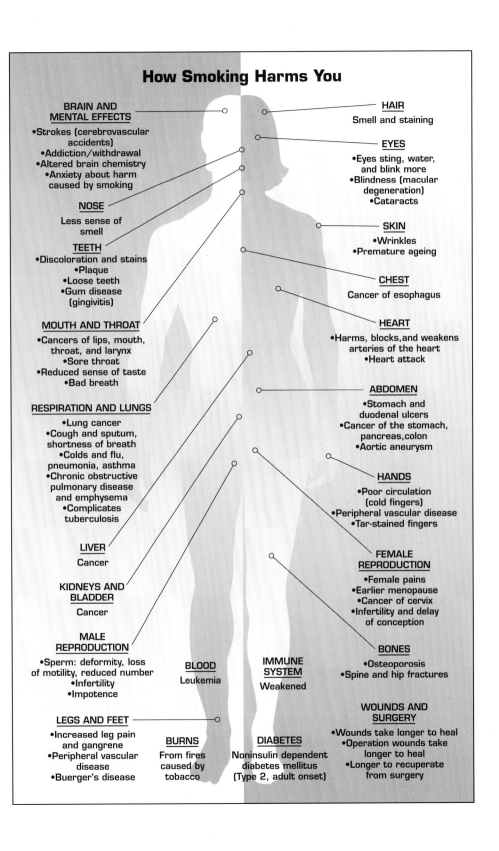

How Smoking Harms You

BRAIN AND MENTAL EFFECTS
- Strokes (cerebrovascular accidents)
- Addiction/withdrawal
- Altered brain chemistry
- Anxiety about harm caused by smoking

NOSE
Less sense of smell

TEETH
- Discoloration and stains
- Plaque
- Loose teeth
- Gum disease (gingivitis)

MOUTH AND THROAT
- Cancers of lips, mouth, throat, and larynx
- Sore throat
- Reduced sense of taste
- Bad breath

RESPIRATION AND LUNGS
- Lung cancer
- Cough and sputum, shortness of breath
- Colds and flu, pneumonia, asthma
- Chronic obstructive pulmonary disease and emphysema
- Complicates tuberculosis

LIVER
Cancer

KIDNEYS AND BLADDER
Cancer

MALE REPRODUCTION
- Sperm: deformity, loss of motility, reduced number
- Infertility
- Impotence

LEGS AND FEET
- Increased leg pain and gangrene
- Peripheral vascular disease
- Buerger's disease

BLOOD
Leukemia

BURNS
From fires caused by tobacco

HAIR
Smell and staining

EYES
- Eyes sting, water, and blink more
- Blindness (macular degeneration)
- Cataracts

SKIN
- Wrinkles
- Premature ageing

CHEST
Cancer of esophagus

HEART
- Harms, blocks, and weakens arteries of the heart
- Heart attack

ABDOMEN
- Stomach and duodenal ulcers
- Cancer of the stomach, pancreas, colon
- Aortic aneurysm

HANDS
- Poor circulation (cold fingers)
- Peripheral vascular disease
- Tar-stained fingers

FEMALE REPRODUCTION
- Female pains
- Earlier menopause
- Cancer of cervix
- Infertility and delay of conception

BONES
- Osteoporosis
- Spine and hip fractures

WOUNDS AND SURGERY
- Wounds take longer to heal
- Operation wounds take longer to heal
- Longer to recuperate from surgery

IMMUNE SYSTEM
Weakened

DIABETES
Noninsulin dependent diabetes mellitus (Type 2, adult onset)

In just ten minutes of smoking, the oxygen supply to the skin is decreased because of narrowing of tiny blood vessels that supply the skin with nourishment. The flawless skin of models in ads for smoking is a contradiction. In reality, smoking robs your skin of *collagen*, the material that keeps your skin elastic. So smokers have more wrinkles than nonsmokers. Of course, the wrinkles don't appear at once, but smokers' faces wrinkle at an earlier age than those of nonsmokers. Smokers get more and deeper wrinkles than nonsmokers.

Have you ever heard of "smoker's face"? You don't want one. Smoker's face is a combination of wrinkles and a grayish pallor. A single cigarette can reduce the blood supply to the skin for more than an hour. It's not surprising that giving up smoking improves the blood supply to the skin and gives it a more natural color.

Teens and preteens who smoke are more susceptible to colds and asthma attacks. About one in three people who are treated for asthma attacks in emergency rooms is a smoker, yet few believe that their smoking had anything to do with their emergencies.[5]

Of course there are also the short-term effects of yellow teeth, smelly clothes, and bad breath, to name a few.

In Case You Want to Know: Some Long-Term Effects

Tobacco has been called the foremost poison of the twentieth century. As the amount of smoking declines in the twenty-first century there may be fewer cases of cancers of the mouth, bronchi, lungs, esophagus, stomach, liver, pancreas, kidney, bladder, prostate, cervix, colon, and other cancers from tobacco use. In addition to these diseases, smoking contributes to many others. Tobacco harms just about every part of the body it touches: on the way in, where blood carries it all around the body, and on the way out.

Long-term effects of smoking are less interesting to most teens than the short-term effects. When you are young it is difficult to be concerned about death in middle age. It doesn't even seem real unless it affects a close relative or someone you know, or if you are looking at an ad from the *Truth Campaign* that shows rows of caskets in front a cigarette company's building.

The World Bank reports that half of long-term smokers will eventually be killed by tobacco, and half of these will die in middle age.[6] The number of people annually who die from smoking is the same as the number of occupants of three 747s crashing every day for a year.

Finding out about health risks from smoking is easy. There are over 70,000 medical articles dealing with the risks of smoking.[7] Although smoking is known to adversely affect nearly every system and organ in the human body, relatively few people know this. In the United States, the warning labels on cigarette packages tell only a few hazards, and most people ignore them. Smokers who are addicted to nicotine pay little attention to the Surgeon General's Warning on the outside of cigarette packs. "Smoking Causes Lung Cancer, Heart Disease, *Emphysema*, and May Complicate Pregnancy" is seldom noticed any more than the bar code.

Complete information about the health risks of smoking is not disclosed the way it is for most drugs. You have probably noticed the page of fine print that follows a magazine ad for a prescription drug, telling of possible side effects of the drug. Have you ever seen a page with fine print stating side effects of smoking on the page following a tobacco ad?

The American Council on Science and Health has published a book, *Cigarettes: What the Warning Label Doesn't Tell You*, with sections on the effect of tobacco use on twenty different systems in the human body. Dr. C. Everett Koop, former surgeon general of the United States, describes this book as an authoritative—and chilling—account of what happens when you smoke.[8]

It is true that some smokers live to old age without any smoking-related illnesses. Suppose you spray an ant nest with insecticide. Some of the ants may still live, but that does not mean that the spray is harmless. Smoking kills rich and poor alike, but it does so differently in developing countries than in others. In the industrial world, smoking generally kills by causing heart attacks and lung cancer, while in developing countries, smoking tends to kill by causing emphysema and liver and stomach cancer. In India, a developing country, a major risk from smoking is tuberculosis.[9]

Heart Diseases

Most people are aware of the connection between smoking and lung cancer. Smoking also plays a major role in heart diseases and high blood pressure. The number of smokers who die from *cardiovascular disease* is equal to or even greater than those who die from lung cancer.[10]

Some studies show that blood pressure returns to normal between cigarettes, but repeated smoking throughout the day results in higher-than-average blood pressure.[11] While high blood pressure can lead to heart problems, swings in blood pressure are even more dangerous and more likely to lead to heart disease. Smoking can also cause irregular heartbeat, a condition that leads to greater risk of heart attack and stroke.

Smoking contributes to heart disease in other ways, too. Toxic chemicals found in cigarette smoke, along with a number of other factors, can damage the lining of the blood vessels leading to the heart. This leads to the formation of scarlike tissues that gives rise to *atherosclerotic plaque*. This and other changes caused by smoking play a role in the two- to four-fold greater incidence of *coronary heart disease* and the 70 percent increase in the death rate from it.[12]

Smokers have more angina and more heart attacks than people who do not smoke. Smokers have about eight times the risk of aortic aneurysms as nonsmokers. In this condition there is a weakening of the wall of the artery that carries blood from the heart to the rest of the body. This may cause a rupture.

The connection between heart disease and smoking has been known for more than sixty years, but many smokers still do not realize there is a connection. Smoking accounts for about one fifth of all deaths from heart disease in the United States and for many more illnesses.[13]

Smokers' Lungs

It's the nicotine that keeps you addicted, but the tar and many other poisons that are present in the smoke cause great damage. Tar, the combustion product in tobacco leaves, exposes smokers to a high rate of lung disease. Smokers cough a lot to clear foreign matter from their tracheas (windpipes) and from bronchi (the tubes that branch out to each lung).

When smoke is inhaled, it irritates and eventually kills the *cilia*, the microscopic hairs that line the tubes that lead to the lungs. These tiny hairs are coated with a thin layer of mucus. Normally, the cilia are in constant motion, propelling the mucus, dust, bacteria, and other foreign particles toward the throat where they are either swallowed or coughed out. Smoking paralyzes the cilia, so dust and air pollutants accumulate and make the lungs vulnerable to *bronchitis*, a disease in which the airways become inflamed and clogged with mucus.

When bronchitis occurs often, the linings of the bronchial tubes thicken. Frequent bouts of bronchitis may lead to emphysema, a disease in which the tiny sacs in the lungs gradually lose their elasticity and the lungs become less able to function. Ninety percent of the people who develop emphysema develop it from long-term smoking. It affects about 1.6 million Americans, usually after continuous exposure to cigarette smoke. Many long-term smokers eventually become short of breath even when they are resting. People who suffer from emphysema may become totally dependent on the oxygen that is delivered to them through tubes in their noses from portable oxygen tanks. You may have seen someone in the nonsmoking section of a restaurant with plastic tubing connected to an oxygen tank on a small cart. There is no cure for emphysema.

When smokers inhale, most of the tars contained in the smoke stay in the mucus that coats the lungs, and this often contributes to lung cancer. Inhaled tobacco smoke damages the cells in the air sacs in the lungs. Some of these cells may form a wartlike cancerous tumor, and as the tumor grows it spreads into other parts of the lungs. From there it may spread into the blood and be carried to bones, the brain, or other organs.

Most teens know that there is a risk of lung cancer from long-term smoking. Before cigarettes became popular, lung cancer was very uncommon, but rates have increased dramatically along with the increase in smoking. It is now the most common form of fatal cancer. Even if you smoke only a few cigarettes a day, you increase your risk of lung cancer.

Lung cancer usually develops slowly. In some cases, especially when it is caught early, it is possible to cure it. Most smokers who develop lung cancer quit smoking after they hear the diagnosis.

Oral Cancer

Any tobacco use can cause *oral cancer*, but smokeless tobacco is especially harmful to the mouth. One of the first noticeable effects of smokeless tobacco use is a white patchy area on the site where the tobacco is placed. The tissue may appear thickened and wrinkled and later become red. This is a precancerous condition called *leukoplakia*.

Smokeless tobacco can lead to cancer of the mouth, *pharynx*, esophagus, and pancreas. It can also cause lung cancer, even though the tobacco does not enter though the lungs. In some cases, the palate grows hard and opening the mouth becomes difficult. Sometimes a part of the jaw and/or part of the tongue has to be removed.

In spite of efforts to spread the word about the effects of smokeless tobacco use, it continues to remain popular. In 2003, concern about the effects of smokeless tobacco brought an announcement by Surgeon General Richard Carmona stating that smokeless tobacco was not a safe alternative for cigarettes.[14]

Cigar smokers often believe they won't have a problem with lung cancer because they don't inhale. But tobacco use affects tissues in the mouth and gums, and many cigar smokers, along with pipe smokers and users of smokeless tobacco, suffer from oral cancer.

Alcohol and tobacco have been described as a deadly duo. Beer, wine, and other alcoholic beverages may cause levels of nicotine to fall more rapidly, and this may be an explanation of why drinkers smoke more than abstainers. The risk of developing cancer of the mouth, lip, tongue, larynx, pharynx, esophagus, and respiratory tract increases much more for people who abuse both nicotine and alcohol than the sum of these two kinds of abuse.[15]

The Search for a
Safer Way to Smoke

The search for a safer cigarette has been long and expensive. Bertram Eichel, a biochemist, developed a filter back in 1969 that removed the most harmful components from cigarette smoke. His work was funded by the Council for Tobacco Research, a now-defunct arm of the tobacco industry that discontinued this funding after he published his research findings. At that time, tobacco companies were afraid to admit that smoking was dangerous, for fear of lawsuits. In 2003, with the health risks of smoking well established, Eichel set up a company, Quest Research Group, to revive his work on safer cigarettes.[16]

Many smokers still wrongly believe that low-tar or light cigarettes are better for them than full-strength cigarettes. As the truth about risks was spreading, the major tobacco companies tried many different approaches to taking the toxins out of tobacco while preserving the taste. They are still trying.

R. J. Reynolds Tobacco Company introduced Premier in 1988 to look like a traditional cigarette but to deliver nicotine without the usual tar. The American Medical Association said Premier was not a cigarette but a drug delivery system that should be banned, and smokers rejected it because they missed the taste of tobacco. Some said smoking Premier was somewhat like smoking blackboard chalk. Premier was removed from the market after a few months.

After six years and nearly a billion dollars of research, Eclipse was introduced to smokers by R. J.

Reynolds. In this cigarette, the burning charcoal tip heated a sheet of tobacco laced with glycerin. It was offered as a smoking alternative that might cause less risk for certain diseases. But when Eclipse was tested in an independent study, it, too, was found to produce dangerous toxins. In 2000, the American Cancer Society called for its removal from the marketplace, saying it might be more lethal than other low-tar cigarettes.[17] But in the summer of 2003, Eclipse was introduced as a new cigarette that "may present less risks of certain smoking-related diseases, has 80 percent less secondhand smoke, and has no lingering odor." Eclipse ads stated, "The best choice for smokers worried about their health is to quit. The next best choice is to switch to Eclipse."[18] Even in 2005, the cigarette was available only at a limited number of stores.

Philip Morris has been working on a new smoking system called Accord since 1999. Jack Nelson, Philip Morris USA's president of operations and technology, announced the first details of the company's research on Accord in 2001. This potentially less hazardous cigarette is a smoking device that heats tobacco instead of burning it. Smokers insert a special cigarette into a hand-held gadget that uses electronics, a heater, and a battery. When Accord was tested, smokers did not show great acceptance, and the company is still working on it to make it more consumer-friendly.

Brown and Williamson, another major tobacco company, is testing Advance Lights, cigarettes with special filters that are claimed to lower the amount of toxins that reach the smoker. They are made from tobacco that is cured in a way that is believed to lower the formation of cancer-causing chemicals. Advance Lights were introduced as having "All of the taste . . . Less of the toxins." Testing will continue.

In 2003, Philip Morris donated millions of dollars to North Carolina State University for a project to map out tobacco's genetic structure. This knowledge could help scientists learn how to alter genes in tobacco so that a new form of it might play a part in producing products that are less harmful. This may be years in the future.[19]

No Smoking

At the present time, some antismoking activists are calling for the end of all tobacco use. For example, in 2003, Surgeon General Richard Carmona said he saw no need for tobacco products in society.[20] Most teens do not smoke, and many of them are joining the fight against tobacco use.

Cigarette smoking is not only the leading cause of preventable death in the United States, it is also the leading cause of early ill health and disability. The nicknames coffin nails, cancer sticks, and evil weed have real meaning today. The problems caused by tobacco use have been called some of the greatest tragedies in human history.[21]

My Smoking and Your Body: Secondhand Smoke

As more restaurants and public places become smoke-free, it is increasingly obvious that smoking is becoming less socially acceptable. Little knots of smokers still huddle in doorways of buildings where they work, and patrons of bars move outdoors in communities that have banned most indoor smoking. Fresh air fills the public places that used to be hazy with smoke. And the remaining smokers, many of them trying to stop, complain about the difficulty of finding a place to smoke, especially on a hot day when they have to leave their air-conditioned comfort or a cold one when they have to bundle up just to go outside for their cigarettes.

Many restaurants are closing smoking areas and making the whole restaurant smoke-free. A survey that measured support of smoke-free restaurants showed that 71 percent of people questioned preferred nonsmoking restaurants and even 41 percent of smokers preferred them.[1] Studies show that making a restaurant smoke-free has not harmed business, as many feared that it would.

Doris's Story

After her husband died, Doris worked as a waitress in a restaurant for twenty years. She had supported her children, helped send them to college, and now she was ready to retire. Before she made plans for a vacation to celebrate her freedom, she decided to get a medical checkup. Doris never smoked, so she was surprised when the doctor told her that her X-rays showed she had lung cancer. He felt that it was probably caused by tobacco smoke. Where Doris worked, there was a haze of smoke most of the day and evening. Doris worked eight hours a day, five days a week. Most of that time, she breathed in some of the cancer-causing chemicals in the tobacco smoke from the many cigarettes that customers smoked before, during, and after their meals. It never occurred to her that the smoke she breathed in from other people's cigarettes would affect her health.

If you don't smoke, or even if you do, you probably feel what happened to Doris was very unfair. Many people feel that what smokers do to themselves is their own business, but what they do to others is a different matter. Enough people have felt this way about *secondhand smoke* to study it thoroughly and help pass laws so that people like Doris won't be exposed to health risks in restaurants, the workplace, or public areas.

A Known Health Risk

In the early 1970s, when smoking was considered socially acceptable, offering someone a cigarette was a way to open conversation. Ashtrays were put in convenient places in living rooms and every table at a restaurant had an ashtray. In those days, only people who had allergies to tobacco smoke and those who had asthma were at all concerned about secondhand smoke.

But as time went on, and more cases like Doris's began to emerge, scientific studies showed many kinds of medical risks for those who breathed secondhand smoke. A number of grassroots organizations began to push for separate areas for smokers in planes and restaurants.

The first scientific evidence of the dangers of secondhand smoke came from a 1981 study by a Japanese scientist, Takeshi Hirayama. He showed that nonsmoking women who were married to men who smoked suffered more lung cancer than those who lived with nonsmokers. Since then, there have been many scientific studies around the world that show the dangers of breathing secondhand smoke. Today, it is known that 3,000 cases of lung cancer are caused by *passive smoking* (breathing in smoke from a smoky environment, rather than from the direct use of tobacco) every year in the United States alone.[2] The Centers for Disease Control and Prevention report that secondhand smoke may cause as many as 35,000 deaths from heart disease each year.[3] And these are just two of the many medical problems caused by tobacco smoke that are recognized today.

Technically the smoke that nonsmokers breathe is called secondhand smoke, but it also is called *environmental tobacco smoke* (ETS). Exposure to this smoke is also called passive smoking or involuntary smoking. The smoke consists partly of *mainstream smoke*, or the smoke that is exhaled by the smoker, and partly of side-stream smoke, or the smoke that is emitted between the puffs of a burning cigarette, cigar, or pipe. When a cigarette is smoked, about half of the smoke generated is side-stream smoke, which contains essentially the same compounds as those identified in mainstream smoke, but in greater amounts. No matter what it is called, numerous studies have shown that exposure to tobacco smoke presents a serious and substantial public health risk.

Passive smoking is the third leading cause of death in the United States each year. Every eight smokers who kill themselves from smoking take one nonsmoker with them.[4] The U.S. Environmental Protection Agency has classified environmental tobacco smoke as a class A carcinogen, along with other known cancer-causing substances such as asbestos, arsenic, benzene, and radon gas.

For many years, smokers scoffed at the idea that their smoke caused problems for others, but now even they know it is a real danger. Nonsmokers are making major changes in society. Before June 2003, Alabama was the only state not to restrict indoor smoking; now all states have some form of regulation to protect non-smokers. Many local governments have laws that are even stricter than state laws. For many years, non-smokers thought they avoided health risks from smoke if they were seated in a nonsmoking area of a restaurant or other room. Separating smokers from nonsmokers in public places has helped to protect nonsmokers to a degree, but it does not eliminate a nonsmoker's exposure to environmental tobacco smoke.

Enough voices have been raised in protest to smoke-filled air to add new laws that make many more places smoke-free. For example, in New York City, where many places were already smoke-free, a ban went into effect on April 4, 2003, that prohibited smoking even in bars. According to *The New York Times*, smokers watched a final haven—bars—close with shrugs and resignation.[5] Four months later, a similar ban on smoking went into effect for New York State. By the fall of 2003, five states had strict laws on prohibiting smoking in most public indoor sites.[6] More than 1,500 communities around the country, including some beach areas, have enacted clean air

---

United States laws that ban smoking in workplaces, public buildings, public transportation, restaurants, and even bars are protecting nonsmoking adults from exposure to the smoke from other people's cigarettes. Adults in other countries, and children of smokers the world over, are not so fortunate. The health effects can be devastating for both as shown in the chart at right.

Harm Caused by Passive Smoking

HEALTH EFFECTS ON CHILDREN

HAIR
Smell

EARS
Middle ear infections
(chronic otitis media)

EYES
Sting, water,
and blink more

RESPIRATION AND LUNGS
•Respiratory infections (including
bronchitis and pneumonia)
•Asthma induction and
exacerbation
•Chronic respiratory symptoms
(wheeze, cough, breathlessness)
•Decreased lung function

HEART
•Deleterious effects
on oxygen, arteries
•Increased nicotine
receptors

BLOOD
Possible association
with lymphoma

BURNS
From fires caused
by tobacco

ROLE MODEL
Greater likelihood of
becoming a smoker
as a teenager

HEALTH EFFECTS ON ADULTS

HAIR
Smell

BRAIN AND MENTAL EFFECTS
Stroke

EYES
Sting, water,
and blink more

NOSE
Irritation

RESPIRATION AND LUNGS
•Lung cancer
•Worsening of pre-existing
problems, such as
asthma, chronic obstructive
pulmonary disease,
emphysema

HEART
•Harms, clogs and
weakens arteries
•Heart attack, angina

UTERUS
•Low birth weight or
small for gestational age
•Cot death or sudden infant
death syndrome (SIDS)
after birth

BURNS
From fires caused
by tobacco

laws, and more laws are expected to go into effect as many smokers and nonsmokers alike enjoy the clear air that makes food taste better and eliminates the health risks of breathing secondhand smoke.

Hundreds of organizations around the country and around the world are fighting to clear the air from secondhand smoke. For example, the British government began using ads on television in July 2003 that showed babies inhaling smoke while playing with toys.[7] Ireland ordered a ban on smoking in workplaces and pubs in 2004. In addition to bans in workplaces, many countries, such as Ireland, Norway, Finland, and the Netherlands, have banned smoking in public places. Some countries in Europe are moving toward adopting American-style bans on smoking in bars.[8]

What Secondhand Smoke Can Do

For some people, a smoke-filled room ruins the taste and smell of food. In crowded restaurants, smoking can produce six times the pollution of a busy highway.[9] Smoke can cause reddening, itching and watering of the eyes, wheezing, and coughing. These are annoying but minor problems compared with the heart attacks and lung cancer mentioned earlier. According to John Banzhaf, executive director of Action on Smoking and Health, over 96 million Americans have chronic health conditions that make them especially susceptible to tobacco smoke. In short, smoke-filled air is not only gross; it's dangerous.

Many kids whose parents smoke are concerned about their parents and the smoke to which their young brothers and sisters are exposed. Secondhand

> You would not give someone permission
> to step on your toes or blow small particles
> of asbestos into the room, so you don't need
> to give anyone permission to fill the air
> around you with noxious fumes.

smoke can increase the number of episodes and the severity of asthma attacks. It causes several hundred thousand lung infections, like pneumonia and bronchitis, in babies and children each year. Because children's bodies are small and still growing, they are affected most by poisons in secondhand smoke. Secondhand smoke is especially harmful to young lungs, making them more vulnerable to infections, and contributing to ear infections. Secondhand smoke is even considered a risk for *sudden infant death syndrome* (SIDS) in babies. Researchers have found higher concentrations of nicotine in the lungs of babies who died of SIDS than in babies who died from other causes.

According to at least one study, being around people who are smoking can increase a woman's risk of contracting breast cancer.[10] Secondhand smoke has the same effect on nonsmokers as on smokers. It is by far the worst source of pollution to which most people will ever be exposed.

Measuring Cotinine

Some progress is being made on reducing the exposure of people to environmental tobacco smoke. This can be tested by checking the presence of a product of nicotine called *cotinine* that forms in the body when a person is exposed to smoke. This chemical persists longer in the body than nicotine. It can be measured in blood, saliva, urine, or hair, but most tests are done on blood. Scientists have tested blood samples of nonsmokers at random for levels of cotinine for more than a decade. In 2002, the United States Centers for Disease Control and Prevention reported that levels of cotinine in nonsmokers' blood have plunged more than 70 percent since the early 1990s. Another study shows that nonsmokers are making progress. Levels of cotinine decreased 75 percent in nonsmoking adults, 55 percent in teens, and 58 percent in children between 1999 and 2000.[11] These studies suggest a dramatic reduction of the general public's exposure to secondhand smoke. However, there are still too many people, especially young people, who continue to be exposed to environmental tobacco smoke.

The Right to Smoke

Does the government have the right to interfere with your tobacco use? "It's my body to do with it what I please." "I can spend my money as I choose." Everyone has heard the complaints from smokers about laws that forbid them to smoke in restaurants and public places. A nonsmoker complains, "I hate the smoke-filled rooms, but what I hate more is the city trying to regulate my personal freedom." But "I'm not hurting anybody but myself," no longer rings true. Smoking is not a personal liberty. It harms others.

"OK, so smoke-filled rooms affect the health of some nonsmokers. Why don't they just go somewhere else?" one smoker argues. A nonsmoker replies, "What about people like Doris who don't smoke, but need to work in smoke-filled places?" Teenage workers are the least likely to be protected against secondhand smoke, since young workers are heavily concentrated in the food service industry.

Almost everyone knows that many smokers have health problems when they get older. But smokers

Numbers Affected by Passive Smoking in the USA Annually During the 1990s

Adults

Lung cancer	3,000
Ischaemic heart disease	35,000 to 62,000

Infants and Children

Low birthweight	9,700 to 18,600
Cot death (SIDS)	1,900 to 2,700
Bronchitis or pneumonia in infants	150,000 to 300,000
Middle ear infection	700,000 to 1,600,000
Asthma induction (new cases)	8,000 to 26,000
Asthma exacerbation	400,000 to 1,000,000

During the 1990s, the numbers of nonsmoking adults and children affected by passive smoking in the United States were disturbingly high. It is hoped that legislative action that took place in the late 1990s and early 2000s will reduce these numbers significantly.

say, "It won't happen to me and, even if I get sick, that's my business." Not everyone agrees with this smoker. In high-income countries, smoking-related illness accounts for between 6 and 15 percent of annual health care costs.[12] Some of this health care will be paid for by taxation, so nonsmokers bear a part of the smoking population's cost, probably far beyond what smokers contribute in tobacco taxes.

Each year, many thousand people die from second-hand smoke.[13] Some insurance experts argue that since smokers tend to die at an earlier age than nonsmokers, their lifetime care costs may be smaller than those of the nonsmokers who live longer. This is controversial, but it is certain that smokers do impose some health damage, nuisance, and irritation on nonsmokers.

A number of reasons are given for the right of the government to interfere with the right of individuals to smoke. In addition to the fact that smoking harms people other than smokers, most children start smoking before they are aware of the many health risks of tobacco and of its addictive nature. The choice to smoke at any age differs from the choice to buy other consumer goods, since smoking is the only consumer product that kills not just the buyer but also others when used as intended. Smoking is not a civil-rights issue. It is a health issue.

The WHO Tobacco Treaty

In May 2003, the World Health Assembly in Geneva, Switzerland, agreed on a global antitobacco treaty. All 192 nations who are members of the World Health Organization (WHO) voted to approve the Framework

Convention on Tobacco Control.[14] This is the first public health treaty adopted globally. Forty nations were needed to ratify the treaty to make it effective and on December 1, 2004, the fortieth nation, Peru, signed the treaty. These forty countries were then able to implement the provisions of the treaty for their countries. According to the World Health Organization, 168 nations, including the United States, have signed it but have not yet ratified it. Signing the treaty shows the governments' interest or intention to become a party at a later time.

The treaty is important for its symbolic value in helping developing countries in their battle against tobacco companies. Now the countries, which have been targeted to replace former smokers in the industrial world, can fight with a united front. Many struggling nations need help in preventing an epidemic of tobacco-related illnesses that will follow a wave of new smokers.

The treaty calls for new restrictions on second-hand smoke, greater action toward the prevention of large-scale smuggling of tax-free cigarettes, and higher taxes on tobacco products. It calls for discontinuing promotions such as dance CDs put out by Marlboro in Hong Kong and the giveaways at rock concerts. Cigarette logos are to be removed from awnings of restaurants, and many other forms of advertising are banned in countries around the world. In addition to tough new rules on advertising, it calls for new rules on marketing and the sale of tobacco products.

Many countries around the world are making efforts to clear the air of tobacco smoke and discourage people from using smokeless tobacco.

Ads: A Reality Check

No one wants to look foolish. Who wants to admit they bought into the ads of the tobacco companies? Who wants to admit they believed the ads that make smoking and smokeless tobacco look great? Even though nobody wants to admit being influenced by them, cigarette ads are apparently successful or tobacco companies would not continue to spend money on them.

The Chewing Gum Story: Selling an Idea

There's an old story about starting a used chewing gum trend. It's really quite awful. Suppose you saw a famous television star picking up used gum and chewing it. Disgusting, right? Then suppose that during the next few months, you saw many ads showing handsome, sexy, independent teens chewing used gum. Some teens look rebellious as they pass previously chewed gum from one to another. There is a television sitcom in which a team of soccer players share some gum at halftime, and football players pass their used gum to others while they sit on the bench. Glamorous people sharing used gum are shown having fun on the beach, riding horses, having parties, wearing beautiful clothing. Do you think you would learn to accept used gum? Still sounds gross? Of course, not many teens would buy into the pitch for chewing used gum. They know it could carry germs. They know it would taste bad. How stupid can people be?

The tobacco companies believe the ads for cigarettes that show attractive young men and women participating in sports, enjoying life to the full while they smoke, will entice teens to smoke. And to some degree they do. Why else would kids start smoking? No one starts smoking for the nicotine in cigarettes; they buy into the false promises of the ads and the pressure from kids who are already addicted. It has been shown that kids are more susceptible to advertising than adults.[1] As further evidence of the impact of ads, most young smokers choose the most heavily advertised brands: Marlboro, Camel, and Newport.[2] The tobacco companies claim that they do not advertise in media that kids have access to, but reports show that some kids as young as three can recognize specific brands of cigarettes.[3]

What the Ads Used to Say

When your grandparents were growing up, not much was known about the harmful effects of smoking. Cigarette ads emphasized full, rich flavor, costlier tobaccos, and a mildness "that's cool and easy on the throat." Camel surveyed doctors and advertised that three national research organizations found that more doctors smoked Camel than any other brand.

Philip Morris admitted that inhaling cigarette smoke increased the chance of throat irritation. It claimed its brand caused less irritation than other brands; the other brands caused irritation that lasted five times as long. With Philip Morris there was "never a worry about throat irritation."

Lucky Strike called on doctors, too, and asked them if they found Lucky Strikes less irritating than other brands. Doctors who answered yes were given several free cartons. An ad followed the survey claiming that "20,679 Physicians Say Luckies are Less Irritating."[4] And if you wanted to smoke without unpleasant symptoms of oversmoking, you could change to Juleps. Ads for this cigarette claimed you could smoke all you wanted without getting a "burned-out throat." "The miracle mint in Juleps freshens your mouth at every puff," according to the ad.[5]

In another ad campaign, you were told to reach for a Lucky instead of a sweet, appealing to women who wanted to remain slim. A competitor suggested that women have a chocolate and a cigarette as a way to relax. By the 1930s, ads encouraged women to smoke in public as a way of asserting women's rights. Cigarettes were presented as torches of freedom.

Every doctor in private practice was asked:
—family physicians, surgeons, specialists...
doctors in every branch of medicine—

"What cigarette do you smoke?"

According to a recent Nationwide survey:

More Doctors
Smoke Camels

R. J. Reynolds Tobacco Company, Winston-Salem, N. C.

than any other cigarette!

THE "T-ZONE" TEST WILL TELL YOU

The "T-Zone"—T for taste and T for throat—is your own laboratory, your proving ground, for any cigarette. For only your taste and your throat can decide which cigarette tastes best to you...and how it affects your throat. On the basis of the experience of many, many millions of smokers, we believe Camels will suit your "T-Zone" to a "T."

Not a guess, not just a trend...but an *actual fact* based on the statements of doctors themselves to 3 nationally known independent research organizations.

Yes, your doctor was asked...along with thousands and thousands of other doctors from Maine to California.

And they've named their choice—the brand that more doctors named as their smoke is *Camel!* Three nationally known independent research organizations found this to be a fact.

Nothing unusual about it. Doctors smoke for pleasure just like the rest of us. They appreciate, just as you, a mildness that's cool and easy on the throat. They too enjoy the full, rich flavor of expertly blended costlier tobaccos. And they named Camels...more of them named Camels than any other brand. Next time you buy cigarettes, try Camels.

Young people will no doubt find this 1950 ad for Camel cigarettes shocking—but at the time it was common practice to use medical endorsements in ads, perhaps to counteract the growing public suspicions about the risks of smoking.

In the early 1930s, health officials began to suspect that smoking was responsible for the rise in the number of cases of lung cancer, a disease that had been uncommon in the past. The first filtered cigarette was introduced in 1936, and many tobacco companies followed this trend. Ads for them emphasized the claim that filtered cigarettes protected smokers' health.

Marlboro, a filtered brand, was first promoted by Philip Morris as a mild brand for women. Later, to increase sales, Marlboro was given a whole new image. It was repackaged in a flip-top box, made with tobacco that was not as mild as before, and was promoted by the now-famous Marlboro man. The rugged cowboy image appealed to the public and Marlboro sales grew. The Marlboro man, Wayne McLaren, who had enticed many young Americans to smoke, developed lung cancer. Three months before he died, he appeared at the annual Phillip Morris shareholders meeting and asked the company to voluntarily limit its advertising. The Marlboro man who replaced him, David McLean, died of the same disease. After the government prohibited the use of the Marlboro man in ads because of its appeal to children, the image of Marlboro Country remained as a place with wide open spaces and smoke-free fresh air. Marlboro continued to be a leader in cigarette sales.

Joe Camel, a well-recognized cartoon character, appealed to people of all ages, but it, too, was banned because of its special appeal to children. Before it was banned, kids as young as six could identify Joe Camel as easily as Mickey Mouse. Joe Camel was so popular that when the ads were banned, *The New York Times*

This scene has a certain irony in that the Marlboro man, handsome as ever, is looking out over a media frenzy taking place on June 20, 1997, the day the tobacco companies and state attorneys-general announced an agreement requiring the companies to pay billions of dollars to the states in compensation for caring for sick smokers.

ran a headline that read: "Advertising: Joe Camel, A Giant in Tobacco Marketing, Is Dead at 23."[6]

Perhaps your parents or grandparents remember the days when television programs had stars who were heavy smokers. Edward R. Murrow and Arthur Godfrey starred in programs in which they always seemed to be smoking a cigarette. But today, tobacco is no longer advertised on radio, television, or billboards. Cigarette ads have been banned from television and radio since 1971. Tobacco companies were forced to stop advertising on billboards in 1998, but ads still appear in adult magazines that kids read and these ads encourage kids to smoke.

Many of the leading popular women's magazines carry articles that warn of the dangers of additives and pesticides in food, problems that affect only relatively small numbers of people. But the same magazines carry ads that make cigarettes look glamorous, fun, sexy, and elegant.

Translating Today's Ads

Many tobacco ads run in adult magazines that kids read. The ads are presented in a way that make you think the one ingredient you need to be like beautiful, popular, athletic people is a cigarette. When you look at an ad for tobacco, notice how it portrays people who smoke. Look very carefully. If it's an ad about sports, does it imply that smoking will make you a better athlete? What is it about the ad that tries to convince you to smoke?

Many ads try to make you believe that if you smoke or use smokeless tobacco you will make more friends, be more desirable, and have more fun. Think about it. Do you think the smelly clothes, bad breath, and yellow teeth of a smoker would make you more desirable? Do you think being short of breath will make you a better athlete? Many ads for tobacco show clean, refreshing scenes. Somehow the smoke from the cigarettes never clouds the air. None of the ads shows the health risks. Fortunately, many of today's teens know that the purpose of the ads is to encourage people to smoke and they are able to look at them realistically. The bad news is that there are still 4,400 kids a day who don't get it—and are influenced to light up their first cigarette.

Have you ever tried to translate an ad to see if tobacco companies are trying to manipulate you? TEENz247, a program of the Winnebago County Health Department of Illinois, has a collection of tobacco ads from the past and today. Its Hall of Fame, called a Hall of Shame, looks at each ad from a realistic teen's point of view, pointing out how teens are being manipulated by big tobacco companies.[7]

When you see tobacco ads in magazines, compare them with the truth. How do the ads portray people? Will smoking actually make them that way? Note where they hide the surgeon general's warning. Notice the placement of cigarette ads in convenience stores.

"Ads" in the Movies

You don't see ads for tobacco in the movies. At least, the attempts to get people to smoke are not called ads, but they work the same way. According to a report published by the Campaign for Tobacco Free Kids, smoking is much more prevalent in movies than in real life.[8] Have you noticed how many times smoking is shown in the movies? Does it seem as if some of the actors and actresses are always smoking ciga-

Does smoking really make you sexy and sophisticated the way ads say it will?
OR
Does it make you stinky and someone most people don't want to be with?

rettes? Studies have shown that the more smoking teens see in the movies, the more likely they are to smoke.[9]

Although tobacco companies are now prohibited from distributing free cigarettes to actresses and actors, the price of cigarettes is not a problem for movie stars. Many of them are addicted to tobacco. Screenwriters know that some movie stars are more likely to play a part if they can smoke while acting. Many actors and actresses feel more comfortable when they have something to do with their hands. Smokers who are addicted to nicotine have a hard time doing without a cigarette during the filming of a scene. And in many movies, smoking helps define a character.

Tobacco use in movies, which was falling in the 1970s and 1980s, increased in the 1990s.[10] One study found that, on average, the twenty top-grossing films featured more than 50 percent more instances of smoking an hour in 2000 than in 1960.[11] The tobacco industry is well aware of the impact of celebrities smoking in movies. Smoking on film has been called better than any ad run on television or in any magazine because the movie audience is not aware that it is seeing an ad. One movie can reach millions of young people in North America and around the world. Reruns and videos send the message to kids that tobacco use is OK, or even desirable.

Young people often emulate celebrity behaviors they see on the screen, from fashions to the use of tobacco. What kids see in movies is statistically linked with what they do. Young people who have been heavily exposed to smoking in movies—where smoking is seen as widespread, socially desirable, and normal behavior—are more likely to smoke. The films obviously do not show the long-term consequences of tobacco use. In *Scene Smoking: Cigarettes, Cinema, and the Myth of Cool*, professionals from the entertainment and health fields discuss real-life choices they have made and what they think about the depiction of tobacco on screen.[12] This video is available to schools from the Centers for Disease Control and Prevention in Atlanta, Georgia.

Young people between the ages of fourteen and twenty-two are reviewing many hundreds of movies, television comedies, and drama series in a program known as "Thumbs Up! Thumbs Down!" After being trained to use a standardized formula for analyzing tobacco-related content, reviewers are assigned to watch specific movies and prerecorded television shows. Data gathered is then released to the public through the media and on the American Lung Association's Web site.[13] It is also analyzed by the University of California at Los Angeles and used as a reference around the world.

Smoke Free Movies, a group of health professionals under the leadership of Dr. Stanton Glantz, a professor at the University of California at San Francisco, urges the entertainment industry to rate films that show smoking without showing the consequences as R films. Some experts believe that scenes with smoking are more harmful to kids than the swearing that gives films an R rating.

Motion pictures and television shows may be make-believe, but they are a real advertising agency and sales force for the tobacco industry. They portray smoking as connected with wealth and power, as fun, exciting, and rebellious, much as the ads of the tobacco companies do. Movies have long been considered a factor in increasing adolescent smoking.

Indirect Advertising

Even in countries where advertising is banned, tobacco companies find ways to publicize their brands among young people. They sponsor concerts by internationally famous musicians so the young audiences will link their heroes with the cigarette brands of the sponsors. In many countries, cigarettes are given away at rock concerts, discos, and shopping malls. Since young people are usually faithful to the brand of cigarette that they learn to smoke, it pays for tobacco companies to get kids to try one free.

Many promotion schemes turn kids into walking billboards for a brand of cigarettes. In Malaysia, where it is illegal to sell cigarettes to anyone under the age of eighteen, kids can buy bags and T-shirts with cigarette company logos. Only about 3.5 percent of Malaysian women smoke, but the rate for teenage girls is 10 percent. Indirect advertising is working there and in many other countries around the world.

In nations where the practice is not banned, cigarette companies not only plaster fences and backboards with ads, they advertise on the athletes and their vehicles as well. This rider in the Australian motorcycle Grand Prix is branded from the top of his head to the bottom of his bike!

Even the Internet is used to lure kids to places where marketing activities are being held. A Web site for a rave or concert may be sponsored by a tobacco company that uses promotions at the event. The company may give away caps, T-shirts, or other items with its logo. In a global survey by the Centers for Disease Control and Prevention, 17 percent of students owned an object with a cigarette brand logo.[14]

According to the Campaign for Tobacco Free Kids, tobacco marketing is like a balloon. You squeeze it in at one end and it increases in another place.[15] Where ads are banned, indirect advertising appears in creative new ways to reach young people, such as high-visibility store displays, price discounts that make cigarettes more affordable to kids, and free gifts with purchase. Store promotions are a highly effective way of reaching kids. The major cigarette companies increased their marketing and promotional expenditures alone to a record of $30.7 million a day in 2001.[16]

Selling a product that kills half the people who use it might seem difficult. But when they see ads showing wide open spaces, lakes, fresh air, youth, and vitality, young kids ask, "How can there be anything harmful in a situation like that?" Smokers know.

BADvertising

Way back in 1986, Bonnie Vierthaler started a program of reconstructing tobacco ads to make them honest. She has changed many ads by replacing sections with silly, gross, and disgusting images to make people realize how tobacco ads are concealing the

Badvertising.org is a great website for poking fun at cigarette advertisers. Here The BADvertising Institute gives the term crush-proof box a new significance!

truth. For example, one ad in what she calls the BAD-vertising program is "Merit Dominates Smoking Testing" with the original top portion of the ad and the lower portion doctored to show two tennis players sitting on a bench. One is holding a pack of cigarettes and suffering a heart attack.

The BADvertising Institute has developed exhibits, posters, billboards, slide presentations, and workshops to immunize kids against tobacco use. There are galleries of BADvertising ads on the Web in which messages have been superimposed to make them honest. You can see some of these on the BAD-vertising Web site.[17] Bonnie Vierthaler reaches large numbers of smokers and kids who are thinking about smoking with this unusual program.

Facing the Truth

Smoking translates into giving up control. In February 2000, the American Legacy Foundation, with money from tobacco lawsuit settlements, launched a national media campaign to raise the awareness of the discrepancy between what tobacco companies are telling teens and what the truth actually is. Under the label TRUTH, dramatic messages began appearing on television, radio, the Internet, and in magazines that expose the truth about tobacco companies.

Teens see ads by TRUTH in cutting edge and in-your-face ads in magazines, on TV, the radio, and on the Internet. These ads do not show smoking as an adult behavior. They don't have "don't smoke" messages that can lead rebellious teens to start smoking. The TRUTH campaign presents the health effects of long-term smoking and the marketing efforts of tobacco companies, and teens are left to make their own decisions about whether or not to smoke. It empowers risk-taking and rebellious teens to act defiantly against a powerful institution of authority, the tobacco industry.

The American Legacy Foundation TRUTH campaign relies on hard-hitting ads, such as one filmed in front of a tobacco company in which teens wear T-shirts numbered from 1 to 1,200. The teens stand together and collapse in unison to symbolize the 1,200 people killed each day from tobacco-related diseases. Ads such as this dramatically show the dangers associated with smoking and using other tobacco products. The TRUTH campaign has been credited with playing a major role in the dramatic decline in the smoking rate.

Learning to look carefully at the truth behind cigarette ads will very likely make you immune to their seductive power. You may even find it easy to reject youth-friendly cigarette flavors such as berry, mocha, coconut, and lime.

The Global View: Tobacco
in the Rest of the World

No one really knows exactly when people started to use tobacco for pleasure, but early use appears to be very limited. Some experts say tobacco was used as long as 8,000 years ago; others claim 6,000 years ago, and some people believe its use started little more than 2,000 years ago.

Nicotine has been found in human remains in several different parts of the world, but most habitual use of tobacco in the ancient world appears to be confined to the Americas. The first tobacco users probably chewed the leaves. Later they may have boiled and strained them and added the liquid to drinking water. The first picture of a man smoking tobacco was found in Guatemala on a pottery vessel that dates from before the eleventh century. He is shown smoking a roll of tobacco leaves tied together with a string made from a plant stem.[1]

Tobacco Use Spreads Around the World

About the time of Columbus, Native Americans were smoking dried tobacco leaves wrapped in either palm leaves or corn husks, or stuffed into hollow reeds. Imagine how strange this looked to the explorers who had never seen smoking. They thought the men were "drinking" the smoke through one end after setting the other end on fire. Many Native Americans smoked tobacco in pipes made of wood, stone, or clay. Much early use of tobacco appears to have been religious. Its magic powers were believed to be many, including curing illness, appeasing the gods, and ensuring a good harvest.

Christopher Columbus and his sailors spread tobacco use to Europe. Columbus wrote in his journal that natives of the New World presented him with a gift of fruit and tobacco. When the gifts were taken back to the ship, the fruit was eaten, but the dried leaves were thrown away because the men did not know how to use them. After the sailors watched the local people, they soon learned to smoke the dried leaves that had a distinct odor. By the time they returned to Europe, many sailors were addicted to tobacco.

Columbus and his sailors took tobacco seeds and dried leaves back to Europe, and the habit of smoking gradually became popular there. Cigars came before paper-wrapped tobacco cigarettes. The first cigarettes may have been made by beggars in Seville, Spain, when they wrapped discarded cigar butts in scraps of paper.

Wherever there was tobacco use, the habit stirred controversy. Clergymen of the time considered it a vice because they sensed tobacco was a mind-altering drug. Given the nature of the addiction, no matter who ordered tobacco users to stop, the orders were ignored.

About the middle of the sixteenth century, Jean Nicot de Villemain, the French ambassador to Portugal, sent seeds of the tobacco plant to the queen of France because he believed it to be useful as a medicine for her migraine headaches. The plant that grew from the seeds was christened *Nicotina tabacura*, and the chemical that is the addictive drug in tobacco was later called nicotine.[2]

By the middle of the sixteenth century, considerable European cultivation of tobacco had begun and its use had spread to many countries. In the 1600s, Jesuit and Portuguese missionaries introduced tobacco to China, which eventually grew into the world's largest tobacco market. Along the sea routes, small tobacco farms developed where sailors were assured of enough tobacco to meet their personal needs as well as for gifts and bartering. Traders and sailors carried tobacco to Japan and many other ports around the world. It also grew in popularity in Russia and in Muslim countries, as well as through the rest of Europe and Asia.

Tobacco became a major crop in some of the American colonies, where its use quickly grew in popularity and it became a major export. Tobacco was widely used as money in the colonies, especially in Virginia, where it was used as currency for 200 years. Asking for the colonists' support for the Revolution, George Washington said, "If you can't send money, send tobacco." Tobacco helped finance the American Revolution by serving as collateral for loans in France.[3]

Tobacco Use Slowed by Controversies

Whether people chewed tobacco or smoked it in pipes, not everyone approved of its use. In 1604, King James I expressed his opinion against smoking in a declaration that ended with the famous pronouncement: "Smoking is a custom loathsome to the eye, hateful to the nose, harmful to the brain, dangerous to the lungs, and in the black stinking fumes thereof, nearest resembles the possible Stygian smoke of the pit that is bottomless." As early as 1621, there were places where the use of tobacco for pleasure was prohibited, often as a safety measure against fires.

In 1633, the sultan of Turkey ordered tobacco users executed by starving them, hanging them, or cutting off their heads. He wasn't concerned about the personal health of his soldiers, but he thought tobacco use reduced their fighting ability. In 1683, a Chinese law declared possession of tobacco punishable by execution.[4]

Over the next century, smoking was both praised and condemned, with some physicians claiming tobacco had value as a medicine and others warning of its harm to the human body. Tobacco was recommended for toothache, halitosis, and a variety of illnesses. It was admitted to be a source of pleasure, but some decried its use, both as a fire hazard and a health hazard.

In some Muslim countries, there were harsh penalties against smoking, ranging from slitting of lips to beheading. The Roman Catholic Church threatened excommunication as a penalty for smoking in church, but some of the clergy and church members got around this by using snuff, powdered tobacco that is inhaled. Snuff caused sneezing, and it was outlawed in the middle of the seventeenth century by the pope, who thought sneezing was too similar to sexual ecstasy.[5]

In 1761, a paper, "Cautions against the Immoderate Use of Snuff," was written by Dr. John Hill, an English physician who associated two cases of cancer of the respiratory tract with snuff.[6] At about this time, snuff was especially popular with aristocrats in Europe—where George III's wife was nicknamed "Snuffy Charlotte."[7]

Mass Production of Cigarettes

Despite a growing awareness of health problems, the amount of smoking in Europe and America grew in the eighteenth century. Small snuff mills in Virginia were the first tobacco factories. Pipe tobacco was still widespread and cigarettes became popular by the end of the century. Cigarettes were still made by the person who smoked them or by hand in factories. Paper was rolled around the tobacco on a flat surface and was pasted to hold the paper in place. Then the cigarettes were hand packaged. A person who was very fast could roll about four cigarettes a minute.

In 1880, a patent for a cigarette machine that used a continuous strip of paper was granted in the United States. This was an important change. Cigarettes were formed, pasted, and cut to lengths automatically, many times faster than could be done by hand. By the end of the first year after the invention of the machine, the largest manufacturer of cigarettes had sold a billion of them.[8]

Cigarette manufacturing has since spread around the world. Five trillion cigarettes are made each year in China, where the government is the largest producer of cigarettes in the world. Two-thirds of the people who make tobacco products work in China, India, and Indonesia.[9]

Smokeless Tobacco

Smokeless tobacco has been used for centuries, but the first chewing tobacco company opened in 1875. Chewing tobacco is often called spit tobacco. Spitting tobacco juice on the ground and the floor was a common, unpleasant practice. In the 1890s, spitting outdoors was banned on the grounds that it was unsanitary. Chewing tobacco was so common then that spittoons were found in homes and stores, and small hand-held spittoons were even carried to church by gentlemen. The habit of spitting tobacco juice is considered just as disgusting today as it was long ago. Most smokeless tobacco users are male, but in south Asia, many women chew tobacco.

The Number of Smokers Increases

Snuff use, pipe and cigar smoking, and the use of chewing tobacco persist, but their use continues to decline. During the twentieth century, cigarettes became the most popular way to smoke, and the number of men who smoked worldwide grew rapidly. The cigarette allows tobacco to be inhaled easily, and it provides a quick smoke. Although the American Red Cross and the Young Men's Christian Association (YMCA) had opposed cigarette smoking, they supplied soldiers who fought overseas in World War I. During World War II, cigarettes were provided free to military personnel with their food.

By World War II, the large numbers of American and European women who had begun to smoke privately in the 1920s no longer suffered from social prejudice. Women smokers became a common sight. As the feminist movement got under way, tobacco companies promoted female smoking with ads, using slogans such as "You've come a long way baby." Slim, sophisticated, competent, and sexually alluring female models appeared in many cigarette ads. The message was, and still is, if you smoke you'll be more like the models. Large numbers of women who wanted to look like the models enjoyed the new longer, extra-slim cigarettes, along with many other women who just found pleasure in smoking. Ads that had special appeal to women contributed to a much larger population of female smokers, especially in the United States and other developed countries. When production of cigarettes became more efficient and advertising increased, cigarette sales rose dramatically in the United States.

A Global Epidemic

Of the world's 6 billion people, at least 1.2 billion are smokers.[10] A billion is such a large number that it is impossible to imagine it. If you started counting one number a second without stopping until you reached a billion, you would finish in 31 years, 259 days, 1 hour, 46 minutes, and 40 seconds. And then you would have to count another two hundred million to get to two tenths of a billion.

Today, and every day, an estimated 15 billion cigarettes are smoked worldwide. Tobacco companies produce 5.5 trillion of them a year.[11] This is the equiv-

Annual Global Cigarette Consumption

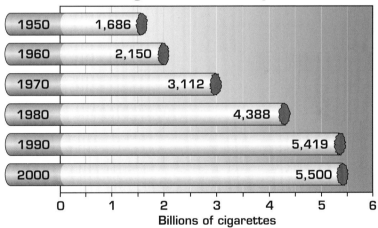

Year	Cigarettes
1950	1,686
1960	2,150
1970	3,112
1980	4,388
1990	5,419
2000	5,500

Billions of cigarettes

The consumption of tobacco is a global epidemic. Tobacco companies are manufacturing cigarettes at the rate of 5.5 trillion a year—nearly 1,000 cigarettes for every man, woman, and child on the planet. Expressed another way, more than 15 billion cigarettes are smoked worldwide every day!

alent of more than two cigarettes per day for every man, woman, and child on Earth. And many people use smokeless tobacco. It takes a huge amount of tobacco to make all these tobacco products, so it is not surprising that tobacco is grown on a wide variety of soils and in many climates.

Many different countries grow tobacco, but two thirds of it is grown in five countries: Brazil, China, India, Turkey, and the United States. Since 1960, much of the production of tobacco has moved from the Americas to Africa and Asia. Its growth has almost doubled in China, Malawi, and the United Republic of Tanzania, while in the United States, where the rate of smoking is declining, many tobacco farmers are turning from tobacco to other sources of income. In 2004, the United States Congress voted for a plan that will help them do so.

In developed countries, where information about health risks is widely spread, fewer people start to smoke and more of them quit than in the past. In the United States in 1950, 45 percent of adults identified smoking as a cause of lung cancer. By 1990, 95 percent of them did. By 2004, only about 22.4 percent of adults in the United States were still smoking cigarettes, and most of them were trying to quit.[12]

Faced with increased regulation of places to smoke and greater awareness of the health risks of smoking in North America and Europe, tobacco companies turned to new markets. During the 1980s, the major cigarette companies convinced the United States government to force countries in Asia to open their markets to imported cigarettes or face trade sanctions. During the 1980s and 1990s, they began marketing heavily outside the United States, especially in developing countries.

Even though many foreign countries produce their own brands of cigarettes, American cigarettes are considered smoother and more pleasant to smoke. This makes a popular market for them far and wide that replaces the diminishing market in countries where the rate of smoking is declining.

China is a large international market that is still growing. Even after China entered the World Trade Agreement in 2001, Chinese tobacco industries continued to supply a large percentage of the cigarettes that are smoked in that country, producing more than 2,500 brands of cigarettes.[13] In 2003, only 3 percent of the market in China was made up of foreign cigarettes that were legally imported. In 2004, Philip Morris announced that it will produce its top-selling cigarettes in China.

The potential market for cigarettes in China is so large that if multinational tobacco companies could supply all the cigarettes, they would have no concern about antismoking activities in other countries.[14] But trade barriers control the market in this huge country, where one of every three smokers in the world lives. Twenty percent of the world's population lives in China and 30 percent of the world's cigarettes are smoked there, mostly by men.[15] The government is attempting to stem tobacco use among young people, but in China, tobacco-related deaths are still very high. The current estimated one million per year may become two million deaths in the year 2025.

India is another country of heavy tobacco use. An estimated 5,500 children start smoking every day and as many as 4 million children under fifteen use tobacco. Bidis, the poor man's cigarette, have been smoked in India for many years and are still popular, along with cigarettes. At one time bidis were made in factories, but cheap labor now supplies much of the demand. In many cases, they are made by children and parents who roll them in their homes. Contractors drop off the tobacco, and a worker scrapes off the stem of a brownish tobacco leaf, sprinkles it with tobacco pieces, rolls it up, tapers both ends, and ties it with pink string. One child can do this in less than a minute and roll as many as a thousand a day, earning money to help feed the family. Gutka, the sweet mixture of tobacco and other ingredients that is placed in the cheek lining of the mouth, is also very popular in India.

Africa is a large market for multinational tobacco companies; in some African countries, more than 45 percent of adults smoke. Although antismoking advocates are trying to make progress, they have far to go. Currently, smoking is generally allowed in most restaurants and bars, public buildings, and even some hospitals in a number of African countries. But more and more no smoking signs are being posted, and several African countries—Uganda, Kenya, and Tanzania—are enacting laws restricting smoking in public places.[16]

Some African countries welcome the money that comes from smokers. Local cigarette manufacture helps supply jobs, and money from cigarette taxes helps pay for care of the sick. In addition to serious financial conditions in many African countries, there are major problems with AIDS, malaria, and malnutrition. Even when the government tries to discourage smoking, it's an almost impossible task. Imagine trying to persuade a man who already has a fatal disease such as AIDS not to smoke.

A number of antismoking advocates in Africa receive backing from groups in the United States. Some African countries are putting health warning labels on cigarette packages, and there is evidence of some progress in reducing the large numbers of Africans who smoke.

The Future of Smoking

As international trade agreements are liberalized, the tobacco market in developing countries grows. Women and children in developing countries are considered relatively untapped markets by tobacco companies. According to a report by the Third World Network, about 15 percent of women in developed countries smoke, but only 8 percent of women in developing countries smoke.[17]

Children and teens make up an illegal, but large, market in many countries. Cigarettes are often sold on the black market as singles or at low prices. Smuggling of tobacco products is very widespread, making up almost a third of all exported cigarettes, an estimated 355 billion cigarettes a year.[18]

The global epidemic of smoking is worse now than it was fifty years ago. With increased smoking and population growth, the number of smokers, according to one estimate, is expected to reach 1.6 billion by 2025.[19] Worldwide, between 82,000 and 99,000 young people start to smoke every day.

Top Five Countries in Cigarette Consumption

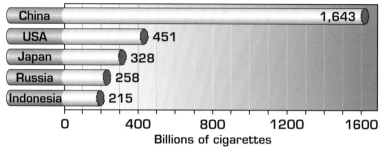

Country	Billions of cigarettes
China	1,643
USA	451
Japan	328
Russia	258
Indonesia	215

Billions of cigarettes

Although cigarette consumption is leveling off in some countries, and actually decreasing in others, people are still smoking more cigarettes worldwide, a trend that is expected to continue. This chart shows the five nations that consume the most cigarettes annually.

To curb the tobacco epidemic, governments should be encouraged to deter children from smoking, provide all people with information about the health effects of tobacco, and protect nonsmokers.[20] While great strides are being made in some areas, the power of nicotine addiction and the appeal of advertisements make the reduction of smoking difficult. No matter what percentage of people stops smoking, it is likely that the last people on Earth will include some tobacco users.

A Corporate View: How
Tobacco Companies Behave

One of the largest public health reform issues in United States history, the war against tobacco companies, traces its origin back to the early 1950s. It has been a difficult battle against a very wealthy and successful industry, one with plenty of legal and public relations resources as well as support from members of Congress from tobacco-growing regions. Over the past fifty years, the effort has come to involve civil lawsuits by individuals, a major settlement between state governments and the tobacco companies, an ongoing federal lawsuit against tobacco companies, regulatory action by the Food and Drug Administration (FDA), class-action suits, and an international antitobacco treaty campaign.

These widespread public health actions were not yet on the horizon when, on December 8, 1953, Dr. Alton Ochsner, president of the American Cancer Society and the American College of Surgeons, made public his prediction that American society was facing disaster unless the smoking and cancer problem was addressed.[1] It was at this time that the public learned that laboratory mice developed cancer when they were painted with a condensed solution of tobacco smoke.

Only one week later, on December 15, 1953, tobacco executives met in New York to oppose and discredit the newly publicized link between cigarettes and cancer. Documents presented as part of the federal lawsuit against tobacco companies show that, even as the industry denied the cigarette-cancer relationship, executives knowingly deceived the public regarding the true dangers of cigarette consumption. In what they called a "frank statement" to the public in 1954, the industry announced that manufacturers did not believe cigarettes harmful.[2] Yet events of the next fifty years tell a different story.

The Story Unfolds

In 1963, a prominent tobacco company lawyer named Addison Yeaman wrote in a secret memo, "Nicotine is addictive. We are, then, in the business of selling nicotine, an addictive drug."[3] In 1964, the United States surgeon general publicly cited health risks associated with smoking, and the following year the Congress required health-warning labels on cigarette packs. Secret evidence from animal studies done in 1970 by the tobacco industry revealed that smoking caused lung cancer.[4]

In 1981, internal tobacco manufacturers' documents showed that executives were aware that young people used their products, and that they were concerned that a future decrease in young smokers would harm their industry financially. In 1982, U.S. Surgeon General C. Everett Koop reported that secondhand smoke might cause lung cancer. The next year, Rose Cipollone, a New Jersey woman who began smoking at age sixteen and later developed lung cancer, filed a case against three tobacco companies. After her death from the cancer, her family continued the case, claiming she was injured by tobacco products. They were eventually awarded $400,000 in damages. In this case, a judge found evidence of a tobacco industry conspiracy, and the documents he obtained provided the public's first glimpse of the internal documents of tobacco companies.

The industry was still denying responsibility in 1990 when smoking was banned on U.S. passenger air flights. In 1992, the U.S. Supreme Court ruled that cigarette pack warning labels do not protect the tobacco manufacturers against lawsuits. In 1994, seven tobacco executives testified before Congress that they believed nicotine is not addictive, but internal industry documents provided contradictory evidence. Later, in 1998, tobacco executives returned to Congress and this time they admitted that nicotine was addictive under current definitions, and that smoking might cause cancer.[5]

In a landmark development in the early 1990s a number of courageous informers from within the tobacco industry came forward with critical information. These sources reported that cigarette makers manipulated the dose of nicotine in cigarettes, leading FDA (U.S. Federal Drug Administration) Commissioner David Kessler to begin a series of investigations. These inquiries showed that genetic research sponsored by the tobacco industry created Y-1 tobacco, a modified form with high levels of nicotine, the seeds of which were illegally exported to Brazil for further development.[6] Kessler's group at the FDA began to look at the possibility of government regulation of nicotine as a drug, since cigarettes essentially serve as drug delivery devices. However, the tobacco industry appealed a lower court decision favoring Kessler's position, and in 2000 the Supreme Court ruled 5–4 that the FDA did not have jurisdiction to regulate cigarettes. A new movement toward FDA regulation reached Congress in 2004, but it did not become law.

The States Fight the Tobacco Industry

Meanwhile, a major effort against the tobacco industry was being mounted on the state level. In 1994, Mississippi State Attorney General Michael Moore began a lawsuit designed to recover from the tobacco industry the costs incurred by his state for the treatment of sick cigarette smokers. Most other states followed his lead over the next four years. Eventually a settlement was reached between the states and the tobacco industry.

The Big Action

During the Clinton Administration, a federal suit was filed that accuses the tobacco industry of fraud and deceptive advertising, marketing, promotion, and warning claims. In this action the United States Department of Justice was trying to prove racketeering charges against five major tobacco manufacturers, and sought damages of $280 billion as well as stricter rules on advertising and warning claims. Even though it was dropped in 2005, the racketeering charge, a tactic typically used by prosecutors against organized crime, was being emphasized because of what the government calls an industrywide conspiracy to place addictive substances in cigarettes.

This suit accuses the tobacco industry of: (1) making false statements about whether smoking causes disease, (2) promoting unsound scientific research to help fight antismoking lawsuits, (3) suppressing research proving the harmfulness of smoking, (4) lying about nicotine as an addictive substance, (5) avoiding the development of safer products, and (6) denying that marketing was directed at youths even while it was trying to capture the young people's market.[7] Part of the reason for the suit was the government's wish to recover some of the $20 billion spent yearly on the federal level to treat smoking-related illnesses. Other goals of the federal suit include support for smoking-cessation programs, stronger advertising restrictions, a citizens' education campaign, and the public exposure of internal tobacco industry documents. After five years of planning, the trial against the nation's biggest tobacco companies opened on September 21, 2004. The trial lasted many month.

More Private Lawsuits

Private lawsuits continue to be filed against tobacco companies, recently for misleading smokers through the marketing of so-called light or low-tar cigarettes, which are no safer than full-strength products. After a victory for the plaintiffs in an Oregon case in 2002, multiple class-action suits have been filed. The trend accelerated after a 2003 decision in an Illinois smokers' class-action lawsuit, in which the judge ordered the Philip Morris Company to pay $10 billion for misleading smokers, thus violating the state's consumer protection laws.[8] In early 2003, there were sixteen class-action lawsuits in 12 states claiming deceptive marketing of light cigarettes.[9]

The Award

Under considerable public pressure, the United States tobacco industry agreed to pay $206 billion to forty-six states, to be disbursed over the course of twenty-five years. In exchange for these funds, the tobacco settlement called for the states to drop health-related lawsuits against the cigarette manufacturers, a major legal and financial threat to the industry. Earlier, $40 billion was awarded to four states under a similar agreement. Apart from the monetary payout to the states, the settlement called for the tobacco industry to spend $1.7 billion to conduct research in the area of youth smoking, and to sponsor antismoking advertising. The industry also agreed to limit marketing directed to children, including the use of cartoon characters, billboard advertising, and the placement of brand names on baseball caps and shirts.[10]

How the Money Is Being Spent

The first installment of the $206 billion tobacco settlement with forty-six states began arriving in local treasuries in early 2000, and was intended to fund antismoking education and to pay for tobacco-related health-care costs. But nothing has prevented individual states from using the money for other purposes, as in Ohio and New Hampshire (public school financing), North Carolina (hurricane damage relief), North Dakota (construction of river levees to prevent flooding), Virginia (road building), and California (prison construction). Other states plan to finance school rebuilding, teacher retirement, and programs to benefit tobacco farmers. Mississippi Attorney General Michael Moore, who began the first state lawsuit against the tobacco industry, terms this behavior "irresponsible," although others reply that the states are simply compensating for years of unbalanced spending on smoking-related health costs.[11]

The National Conference of State Legislatures reported that in their 2003 budgets, thirty-seven states allotted 28 percent of the tobacco funds to health services, 5 percent to long-term care, and 3 percent to children and youths.[12] Despite tobacco settlement money and increased cigarette-related taxes, an independent analysis found that most states were not providing adequate funding for smoking prevention and cessation programs. Recent state budget deficits have made the situation even worse. Some states are using settlement money to balance general budgets. According to the campaign for Tobacco Free Kids, only four states—Maine, Delaware, Mississippi, and Oklahoma—are funding programs at a level advised by the Centers for Disease Control (CDC), and only eight other states at half the recommended funding level.[13] These trends are very disappointing from a public health viewpoint. Many states have cut funding for their tobacco prevention programs and some have completely eliminated them.[14]

Although costly to the tobacco industry, the Master Tobacco Settlement ended the threat of further lawsuits from the states, presumably allowing the tobacco industry a more predictable business environment on a national and international level. The war against the tobacco industry has worsened the public relations problem for corporations already widely seen as purveyors of deadly, addictive substances. The need to fix the industry's bad image is reflected in the Philip Morris Company's change of name to The Altria Group in early 2003.[15] Critics have charged that this industry leader is simply trying to dissociate itself from the idea of tobacco and improve its appearance by changing its name without changing its behavior. At the same time, the company finally has admitted a tobacco-cancer link and has created an Internet Web site devoted to providing health information about tobacco and how to keep it away from young people. Some of these youth anti-smoking ads are accused of making kids more likely to smoke. For example, Philip Morris's "Think. Don't

Smoke." is considered a wolf in sheep's clothing by the American Legacy Foundation.[16]

Whether these industry measures represent a true change of direction in favor of the health of the public or just another cynical manipulation designed to keep the cigarette business prospering is a judgment that must be left to future observers. As Dr. David Kessler observed, because the industry is so powerful financially, it will take more than legislation or litigation before a public health victory can be achieved. Rather, a fundamental change in attitudes and behaviors will be needed, so that one day a product that kills people when used as intended will no longer be socially acceptable, especially among the young.[17] This change is beginning to happen.

Now That I'm Informed:
Some Ideas for Quitting

"Giving up smoking is the easiest thing in the world. I know. I've done it thousands of times."[1] This quotation, and variations of it, are often wrongly attributed to Mark Twain, but the idea is a good one. The comment could be made by many smokers, chewers, and dippers today.

Quitting is easier for some people than others. You may have a friend who says, "I quit cold turkey. All it takes is willpower." Other friends may tell you it is the hardest thing they ever did. Whether you quit on your first attempt or on your fifteenth, you can do it. There are many programs that can help. Some are better for one person than another, but if the first one doesn't work for you, try a different one.

Are You a Nicotine Addict?

Many people know that the drug that makes quitting so hard is nicotine. It is one of the most highly addictive drugs, a drug that is as addictive, or even more so, than cocaine and heroin for some people. "Cigarettes are highly addictive. Studies have shown that tobacco can be harder to quit than heroin or cocaine," is one of the warnings on some Canadian cigarette packages.

Most smokers do not think of themselves as addicts. If you are a smoker or use smokeless tobacco, consider this Hooked on Nicotine checklist:[2]

1. Have you ever tried to quit but couldn't?

2. Do you smoke now because it is really hard to quit?

3. Have you ever felt you were addicted to tobacco?

4. Do you ever have strong cravings to smoke?

5. Have you ever felt as if you really needed a cigarette?

6. Is it hard to keep from smoking in places where you are not supposed to?

7. When you tried to stop smoking (or when you haven't used tobacco for a while), did you find it hard to concentrate?

8. When you tried to stop, did you feel more irritable because you couldn't smoke?

9. When you tried to stop, did you feel a strong urge to smoke?

10. When you tried to stop, did you feel restless, nervous, or anxious because you couldn't smoke?

If you answer yes to any of these questions, you have symptoms of dependence on nicotine. You are "hooked."

Cutting Down?

Many smokers say they are just social smokers. They have one or two cigarettes a day, and maybe one after dinner. Why should they quit? There's no harm in what they are doing. Right? Strangely enough, new reports show that one or two cigarettes a day may do as much harm to your heart and blood vessels as heavy smoking. Just a single cigarette can limit the ability of the blood vessels to dilate, and this is the first step toward dangerous plaque buildup. According to John Ambrose, medical director of St. Vincent's Medical Center in New York City, light smokers show the same damage as heavy smokers.[3]

According to the Centers for Disease Control and Prevention, reducing tobacco use by half or more without quitting did not decrease mortality rates from tobacco-related diseases compared with people who smoked fifteen cigarettes a day.[4]

Even if you are a light smoker, this chapter is for you, too.

The Quit List

Even though young people don't worry much about the long-term health risks of smoking, most young smokers want to quit. You may have your own special reasons, but here are some reasons teens give for wanting to stop smoking or using smokeless tobacco:

- I'm tired of trying to hide my smoking stink with mints, perfume, and body lotion.

- I'm tired of smelling like an ashtray.

- Most teens would prefer to date nonsmokers.

- I've developed a cigarette cough.

- I hate spending so much money on cigarettes. (Money is one of the most common reasons for quitting. Higher taxes on cigarettes are highly effective in reducing the demand for cigarettes.)

- When I run out of cigarettes, life's almost unbearable until I get one.

- I want to be able to run without gasping for breath.

- I've lost my sense of smell.

- I'm tired of having to find a place to smoke.

- I'm tired of burn holes in my clothing.

- People treat me like a leper.

- I'm tired of being a slave to cigarettes.

- Smoking can be dangerous. My grandmother has lung cancer.

- I don't want to get smoker's face (a face that is slightly gray, with wrinkles).

- My teeth are yellow from smoking. I want to get them white.

When you decide your reasons for quitting, make a list. Copy it and post it where you see it often and carry a copy with you at all times. Look at the list every time you feel like smoking. Some programs suggest you look in the mirror while you recite the list many times.

Quitting Is Hard to Do

In its booklet, "Links to Sources of Information about Quitting Smoking," Philip Morris, producer of Marlboro and other popular brands, admits that smoking is addictive. This is what appears under a section on health issues: "We agree with the overwhelming medical and scientific evidence that cigarette smoking is addictive. It can be very difficult to quit smoking, but this should not deter smokers who want to quit from trying to do so." On the opposite page in the booklet, one finds a quote from the United States Food and Drug Administration. "A smoker who makes a serious attempt at quitting smoking has a less than 5 percent chance of being off cigarettes a year later." Smoking is so highly addictive that close to 90 percent of smokers who try to quit have to try more than once.

Here are some suggestions that may help you quit:

Choosing a Quit Day

Quitting may be easier if you plan ahead. Millions of people quit for a day or longer on the day celebrated as The Great American Smokeout that is held annually on the third Thursday of November. Knowing that so many other people are giving up smoking the same day that you are can help you to quit. This event was sponsored by the American Cancer Society in California in 1976, and it became national the next year. Since then attitudes about smoking have changed dramatically, and it is now cool to quit.

Another popular quit day is World No Tobacco Day. This is sponsored by the World Health Organization to call attention to the seriousness of the impact on health. Each year on May 31, national and local efforts are organized to build public awareness, interest, and action. These differ from country to country, but there usually are many media stories that focus on individual tobacco users who quit tobacco use and the strategies that helped them succeed.

Independence Day is also a popular time to quit. You can be free from a product you know you are being manipulated to buy. Or perhaps you prefer New Year's Day or your birthday. Choose a day that is not more than two weeks away, even if it is not a special event other than the day you choose to quit. You can celebrate it every year.

Five Days Before Quit Day

Planning ahead for "quit day" is one of the common suggestions in many of the quit smoking programs.

Five days before you plan to stop, keep a journal of when you smoke and why. Note the things that seem to "go with a cigarette," such as drinking coffee, talking on the phone, being with other smokers, and driving.

Stop buying cigarettes.

Tell your family and friends you are planning to quit. Ask them to understand your changes in mood when you quit. Remind them and yourself that it won't last long. The worst will be over in two weeks.

Common Symptoms of Smoking Withdrawal

Feeling nervous or restless

Feeling depressed

Insomnia

Slower heartbeat

Feeling frustrated or cranky

Feeling hungry

Four Days Before Quit Day

Think of things to hold in your hand instead of a cigarette. If you plan to use cinnamon sticks, now is the time to buy them. Find them in the spice section at the supermarket. You can chew on them, inhale through them, and handle them like a cigarette.

Plan new routines that will help you avoid *triggers*.

Three Days Before Quitting

Make plans for spending the money you save by not smoking.

Make a list of numbers you can call if you need help and put it in a convenient place. You can find some helplines on page 118.

Two Days Before Quitting

You may want to consider the use of *nicotine replacement therapy* such as a patch, gum, inhaler, spray, or lozenges. Many of these therapies have not been tested on young people and some doctors hesitate to prescribe or recommend them. The FDA prohibits the sale of nicotine products to individuals under eighteen years of age without a prescription, so you must see your doctor in order to obtain them. Just as it is against the law to sell cigarettes to anyone underage, it is against the law to sell *nicotine patches* or other products used by adults for nicotine replacement therapy to anyone younger than eighteen without a doctor's prescription.

Nicotine Replacement Therapy (NRT) provides a substitute source of nicotine without the harmful effects of other chemicals in cigarette smoke. NRT makes it easier for smokers to quit, especially if they smoke a pack a day or more. The amount of nicotine in these products kills the cravings but is too small to produce a high. It is absorbed more slowly than from cigarettes and the patch or other nicotine dose is reduced as the treatment progresses. This treatment usually lasts about three months.

If you are going to use NRT, buy the product now. If it seems expensive, remember that you will only use it for a short time.

Another product that claims to help end the smoking urge is called Endit. It is advertised as having tobacco flavor but no tobacco, and it looks like a cigarette. Endit is available in some drugstores, clubs, and restaurants in some large cities on the East and West coasts of the United States.

One Day Before Quitting

Get rid of all the cigarettes from drawers where they are normally stashed, your pockets, and any place where you keep a supply. If you do not get rid of all your cigarettes before quit day, you will be tempted to "use them up," or find a reason for using them, such as preventing waste or satisfying a craving by having just one cigarette.

You can enjoy shredding the last few cigarettes over the toilet and reminding yourself that you will now be in control of your life.

Put away all the ashtrays, lighters, and other things that might tempt you to light up.

Air your room, clean your clothes and do as much as possible to get rid of the tobacco smell. If other people in your house or dorm smoke, ask them not to smoke in front of you. Plan to leave the room when others around you smoke.

Quit Day

Make a note and put it where you will see it frequently: Psychological and social dependence can last a lifetime but the strong urge to smoke a cigarette will pass in about four, five, or ten minutes at the most. Drink a glass of water, chew gum, or take a short walk until the urge passes.

- Stay busy.

- Change your routine.

- Hold a pencil, a water bottle, a paper clip, or something to replace a cigarette.

- Drink a lot of water and fruit juice. Wine, beer and other alcoholic beverages can trigger smoking. After meals, when you usually had a cigarette, take a walk. Brush your teeth.

- Remember that most people don't smoke. Try to stay near nonsmokers.

- Start some new activities that keep your hands busy.

- Write a letter, do crossword puzzles, exercise.

- Spend some time in the library, a museum, a movie theater, or another place where smoking is prohibited.

- Call a supportive friend.

When You Crave a Cigarette

Most cravings are short-lived. They generally fade away in ten to thirty minutes. Handle the craving you are having and don't think about the cravings you might have in the future.

- Go to a different place.

- Change what you are doing.

- Wash your hands.

- Take a shower or a bath.

- Take several deep breaths. Exhale each one slowly.

- Remember that cravings are short-lived.

- Don't smoke just one or even take a puff.

The well-liked movie star, Kirk Douglas, wrote in *The New York Times* about the way he quit. He told how his father carried one cigarette in the breast pocket of his shirt. When he felt the urge to smoke again, he would take it out of his pocket and talk to it. He would ask the cigarette, "Who is stronger? You—me?" Although his father did not stop soon enough to prevent his lung cancer, Kirk Douglas used the same method to quit smoking in 1950 and is an advocate of not smoking.[5]

What Happens to Your Body When You Quit Smoking?

- After twenty minutes, your blood pressure drops to a level close to what it was before you had your last cigarette. The temperature of your hands and feet increases to normal.

- After eight hours, the carbon monoxide level in your blood drops to normal.

- After twenty-four hours, your chance of a heart attack decreases.

- After two weeks to three months, your circulation improves. Your lung function increases up to 30 percent.

- After one to nine months, coughing, sinus congestion, fatigue, and shortness of breath decrease; cilia (delicate hairs) in your lungs regain normal function, increasing the ability to handle mucus, clean the lungs, and reduce infection.

- After one year, your chance of having a heart attack is cut in half.

- After ten years, your risk of dying from lung cancer is about half that of a continuing smoker; risks of cancer of the mouth, throat, esophagus, bladder, kidney, and pancreas decrease.

- After fifteen years, your risk of coronary heart disease is that of a nonsmoker.[6]

- After fifteen years, stroke risk is reduced to that of a nonsmoker.

Some Quick Rewards of Quitting Tobacco Use

Food tastes better. Running up the stairs and other ordinary activities no longer cause shortness of breath.

Your sense of smell improves, and the way you don't smell is appreciated by your friends.

Your nonsmoking friends are glad you quit. You can join a group who thinks smoking is disgusting.

You no longer feel manipulated by tobacco company ads.

Smokeless Tobacco

Most of the suggestions for quitting cigarettes apply to smokeless tobacco. Some communities have a "Through with Chew Week" that was established in 1989 and is still sponsored by their local health departments. You may find a listing for your local health department or quit smoking programs in your telephone book. You may also find help in quitting smokeless tobacco from organizations listed on pages 117–118.

Some smokeless tobacco users find Mint Snuff, pouches made from mint instead of tobacco, helpful. They act as a placebo to help deal with the social and behavioral aspects of giving up chewing tobacco. Mint pouches have no salt or sugar, no tobacco, and no nicotine. Even some smokers find them helpful when they are trying to fight the urge to light a cigarette.

Support Is a Big Plus

Matt Strekel, a senior at Wheaton College in Massachusetts, smoked a pack of cigarettes a day for five years. He figured he had spent about $4,100 on cigarettes. In November of his senior year, he stumped out his last cigarette and quit cold turkey on the day of the Great American Smokeout. He publicized his plans to quit by dressing like a Thanksgiving turkey and challenging the college community to make bets that he would stay smoke free at least through graduation. The money he raised by bets against his goal went to his favorite charity.

Matt said he was really sick of smoking. He didn't want to enter the real world after graduation as a smoker. Knowing that other people on campus were keeping a watchful eye on him helped him avoid lighting up and helped him meet his goal.[7] When he graduated in May 2003, he was smoke free.

Support is one of the most important factors in staying away from nicotine. In a study of the effectiveness of telephone *quit lines*, researchers at the University of California at San Diego found that those who were counseled through their quit line stopped smoking at twice the rate of those who did not seek such help.[8] More than two thirds of the states have quit lines. Certainly, it is easier to quit if you don't try to do it alone. Research from two smoking cessation Web sites shows that the quit rate achieved through Internet-based stop smoking programs may be as high as from traditional programs where the support is face to face.[9] Many smokers find it is easier to quit on the second or third attempt.

There are many quit programs on the Internet and in booklet form. Look on pages 117–118 of this book for a list of Web sites and phone numbers where you can get help in quitting. Check a number of them to see which one appeals most to you.

A Promising Vaccine and Drug

There's promise of an *antismoking vaccine*. NicVAX is still being tested for its safety and effects in humans and it may not be ready for market for years. This vaccine was designed to stimulate the immune system to produce antibodies that bind to nicotine, making them too large to cross the blood/brain barrier.[10] NicVAX may someday be used to prevent nicotine addiction, somewhat the way vaccines are used to protect you against polio, tetanus, and measles. People who are vaccinated against nicotine addiction would not find cigarettes, snuff, spit tobacco, or other tobacco products rewarding, so they would not continue to use them. In 2004, Nabi Pharmaceuticals, based in Boca Raton, Florida, completed trials of another smoking vaccine that could be on the market in as little as two years.

Varenicline, a new drug, was inspired by a natural remedy tested by doctors in the Soviet Union in the late 1960s. Varenicline is an oral medicine that enabled half of the people in the trial to quit smoking after seven weeks, compared with 16 percent who were given sugar pills.[11] This drug, being tested by Pfizer, Inc., is still experimental.

You Are Not Alone

Nearly three-quarters of the 45 million Americans who smoke want to quit. You can be one who succeeds.

Glossary

acetone: a colorless liquid used as a solvent; a toxin found in cigarette smoke.

acetylcholine: A neurotransmitter involved in carrying messages between nerve cells.

addiction: an uncontrollable craving, seeking, and use of a substance such as nicotine or other drug.

ammonia: a common household chemical; a chemical found in cigarette smoke.

amphetamines: illegal drugs, stimulants.

antismoking vaccine: a vaccine to prevent the rewards of nicotine and help people stop smoking.

atherosclerotic plaque: deposits that form inside blood vessels.

bidis: small, brown, hand-rolled cigarettes.

bronchitis: a disease of the respiratory system.

carbon monoxide: a chemical in cigarette smoke that combines with oxygen-carrying molecules in the blood.

cardiovascular disease: a disease of the heart or blood vessels.

cilia: microscopic hairlike structures that help move air along tubes that lead to the lungs.

clove cigarettes (kreteks): contain about 60 percent tobacco and 40 percent cloves.

cocaine: an illegal drug, a stimulant.

collagen: material in human skin that keeps it elastic.

cotinine: a product that forms in the body when a person is exposed to tobacco smoke.

coronary heart disease: a heart condition caused by a problem in the artery that carries blood to the heart.

craving: a powerful, often uncontrollable, desire for drugs, such as nicotine.

cyanide: a poison found in cigarette smoke.

dopamine: a neurotransmitter present in regions of the brain that regulate movement, emotion, motivation, and the feeling of pleasure.

emphysema: a lung disease in which tissue deterioration results in increased air retention and reduced exchange of gases. The result is difficulty in breathing and shortness of breath.

environmental tobacco smoke: secondhand smoke.

formaldehyde: A chemical used in preserving animal tissue; a toxin found in cigarette smoke.

gene: a basic unit of heredity that directs the construction, operation, and repair of living tissue.

gutka: a form of smokeless tobacco.

hemoglobin: a pigment in red blood cells that transports oxygen from the lungs to tissues where oxygen is readily released.

heroin: an illegal sedative drug, prepared from morphine, used by drug abusers.

hookah: a water pipe. Tobacco is drawn through the water in the pipe and inhaled through a long tube on the side of the pipe. Cut, shredded tobacco moistened with a sweetener is kept in the bowl of the pipe and burned with charcoal.

hydrogen cyanide: a chemical found in cigarette smoke that is toxic to humans.

kreteks: see clove cigarettes

leukoplakia: a disease of the mouth and gums that can be caused by the use of smokeless tobacco.

light cigarettes: cigarettes made with low tar and nicotine.

magnetic resonance imaging (MRI): a form of imaging that shows soft tissue.

mainstream smoke: smoke that is exhaled by the smoker.

marijuana: an illegal drug that is smoked, commonly known as pot.

mercury: a metallic element, sometimes known as quicksilver, that is part of a compound found in cigarette smoke. It is poisonous to the human body.

monoamine oxidase (MOA): an enzyme that is involved in the breaking down of dopamine.

neurotransmitters: chemicals that carry messages between nerve cells.

nicotine: a poisonous volatile alkaloid derived from tobacco and responsible for the addictive effects of tobacco. At first it stimulates (low doses) and then it depresses (large doses).

nicotine patch: a patch used to relieve withdrawal symptoms. It is placed on the skin to release nicotine slowly into the body.

nicotine replacement therapy (NRT): products that help relieve some of the symptoms of withdrawal from cigarettes or smokeless tobacco.

nitrosamines: cancer-causing chemicals.

oral cancer: a disease characterized by abnormal cell growth in the mouth.

passive smoking: breathing secondhand smoke.

pharynx: the cavity at the back of the nose and throat.

quit line: a toll-free hotline staffed by counselors who are trained to help people give up smoking.

secondhand smoke: tobacco smoke that is breathed by someone who is not smoking.

smokeless tobacco: tobacco that is used in a form that is not smoked. Chewing tobacco and snuff are the two main forms used in the United States.

snuff: a form of smokeless tobacco. Moist snuff is taken orally; a small amount of ground tobacco is held in the mouth between the cheek and the gum. Dry snuff is powdered tobacco that is usually inhaled, but is sometimes taken orally.

spit tobacco: chewing tobacco.

sudden infant death syndrome (SIDS): one of the leading causes of infant death in the United States. Unexpected death, with infants showing no indication of disease.

tolerance: a condition in which higher doses of a drug, such as nicotine, are required to produce the same effect as that derived from initial use.

trigger: something that initiates a reaction, such as a cigarette craving.

Truth Campaign: a national media campaign by the American Legacy Foundation to raise awareness about tobacco.

withdrawal: the syndrome of physical and psychological symptoms that follows the discontinuing of an addictive drug such as nicotine.

Further Reading

Books and Articles

American Cancer Society. "Kicking Butts: Quit Smoking and Take Charge of Your Health." American Cancer Society, 2002.

Brandt, Allan. *The Rise and Fall of the Cigarette*. New York: Basic Books, 2004.

Brigham, Janet. *Dying to Quit: Why We Smoke and How We Stop*. Washington, D.C: John Henry Press, 1998.

Glantz, Stanton A. *Tobacco War: Inside the California Battles*. Berkeley: University of California Press, 2000.

Heyes, Eileen. *Tobacco U.S.A.: Behind the Smoke Curtain*. Brookfield, CT: Twenty-First Century Books, 1999.

Kessler, David. *A Question of Intent: The Great American Battle with a Deadly Industry*. New York: Public Affairs, 2001.

Krogh, David. *Smoking: The Artificial Passion*. New York: W.H. Freeman Company, 1991.

Lukachko, Alicia. *Environmental Tobacco Smoke: Health Risk or Hype?* New York: American Council on Smoking and Health, 1999.

MacDonald, Joan Vos. *Tobacco and Nicotine Drug Dangers,* Berkley Heights, N.J.: Enslow Publishers, Inc., 2000.

Mackay, Julia, and M. Eriksen. *The Tobacco Atlas.* Geneva: World Health Organization, 2002.

Meister, Kathleen, editor. *Cigarettes: What the Warning System Doesn't Tell You.* New York: American Council on Science and Health, Second Edition, 2003.

Parker-Pope, Tara. *Anatomy of an Industry: From Seed to Smoke.* New York: New Press, 2001.

Surgeon General's Report on Smoking, 28 reports from 1964 to 2004. http://www.cdc.gov/tobacco/sgr/sgr_2004/Factsheets/11.htm

Organizations and Web Sites

Americans for Nonsmokers Rights
www.no-smoke.org

Action on Smoking and Health
www.ash.org

Alliance for Lung Cancer Advocacy, Support, and Education
www.alcase.org

American Cancer Society
www.cancer.org

American Heart Association
www.americanheart.org

American Legacy Foundation
www.americanlegacy.org

The BADvertising Institute
www.badvertising.org

Campaign for Tobacco-Free Kids
www.tobaccofreekids.org

Centers for Disease Control and Prevention
Office on Smoking and Health
www.cdc.gov/tobacco

Join Together Online
www.jointogether.org

National Alliance for Hispanic Health
www.hispanichealth.org

National Association of African Americans for Positive Imagery
www.naaapi.org

National Latino Council on Tobacco and Health Prevention
www.nlcatp.org

National Spit Tobacco Education
www.nstep.org

National Tobacco Information Online Systems (NATIONS)
apps.nccd.cdc.gov/nations/

Oral Cancer Foundation
www.oralcancerfoundation.org

Smoke Free Movies
www.smokefreemovies.ucsf.edu

Tobacco Free
www.tobaccofree.org

Tobacco News and Information
www.tobacco.org

Tobacco Related Diseases Research Program
www.trdrp.org

United States Surgeon General
www.surgeongeneral.gov/tobacco

World Health Organization's Tobacco Free Initiative
www.who.int/tobacco/en

American Cancer Society's Resources
www.cancer.org/docroot/PED/ped_10_3.asp?sitearea=PED
- Cancer Prevention and Early Prevention Facts and Figures
- Plan Your Quit Day
- Complete Guide to Quitting
- Help For Cravings
- Telephone Quit Lines Succeed Where Other Methods Have Failed

American Legacy Foundation
www.americanlegacy.org

American Lung Association
www.LungUsa.org
- Teens Against Tobacco
- Freedom from Smoking

Centers for Disease Control and Prevention
http://www.cdc.gov/tobacco/how2quit.htm.
- Don't Let Another Year Go Up in Smoke: Quit Tips
- I Quit!: What to Do When You're Sick of Smoking, Chewing or Dipping

National Cancer Institute
www.cancer.gov

Nicotine Anonymous
www.nicotine-anonymous.org

Oral Cancer Foundation
www.oralcancer.org

Quitting Tips by Patrick Reynolds
www.tobaccofree.org

The Quit Net
www.quit.org

You Can Quit Smoking
www.smokefree.gov

A guide to many smoking cessation sites can be found at www.about.com. Enter "smoking cessation" in the search box.

Phone Help
For free copies of publications on quitting, call:

Agency for Healthcare Research and Quality
Telephone: 800-358-9295

Centers for Disease Control and Prevention
Telephone: 800-CDC-1311

National Institutes of Health
National Cancer Institute
1-800-4 Cancer

To talk to an expert for local quit line phone numbers, consult: www.smokefree.gov

Chapter One

1. http://www.cdc.gov/tobacco/research_data/youth/Youth_Factsheet.htm
2. J.R. DiFranza and others, "Development of Symptoms of Tobacco Dependence in Youths," Tobacco Control; 11:228–235, 2002.
3. "Tobacco Infection and Prevention Source," http://www.cdc.gov/tobacco/issue.htm.
4. Patricia Zickler, "Adolescents, Women, Whites More Vulnerable Than Others to Becoming Nicotine Dependent," NIDA Notes, Volume 16, Number 2, May 2001.
5. "The First Cigarette" http://www.sfact.com/dohanyzastrol/ a2doc.html.
6. Lisa Henriksen and Christine Jackson, "Children's Body Image Concern and Smoking Initiation: A Prospective Study," http:// apha.confex.com/apha/128am/techprogram/paper_7344.htm.
7. Deborah Pettibone, "Smoking Initiation Linked to Adverse Childhood Experiences." http://www.Roswellpark.org/news.asp?lid=1779&reflid =1778.
8. "Genetic Variation in Serotonin System May Play a Role in Smoking Initiation," NIDA Notes, Vol. 17, No.2 , 2002.
9. www.monitoringthefuture.org/data/04data.html#2004data-cigs
10. Ibid.
11. "Teen Smoking Dropped Dramatically in 2002," NDA Notes, Vol. 17, No. 6, March 2003
12. "The Evil Weed Snuffed Out," *The Economist*, January 4, 2003, p. 22
13. "Teen Smoking Declines Sharply in 2002," http:// monitoringthe future.org/pressreleases/02cigpr.pdf
14. ww.monitoringthefuture.org/data/04data.html#2004data-cigs
15. Ibid.

Chapter Two

1. "Anatomy of a Cigarette" http://www.pbs.org/wgbh/nova/cigarette/anat_ text.html
2. Steve Heilig, "A Pack of Lies: There's No Such Thing as 'Safer Smoking'," *San Francisco Examiner*, December 7, 2001.
3. National Institute on Drug Abuse Research Series, "Nicotine Addiction." 1998, p. 2.
4. David Krogh, *Smoking: The Artificial Passion*. New York: W.W. Freeman, 1991, p. 29.
5. Darryl Inaba, William Cohen, and Michael Holstein, *Uppers, Downers and All Arounders*, Third Edition, Ashland, Oregon: CNS Publications, 1993, p. 120.
6. David P. Friedman and Sue Rusche, *False Messengers: How Addictive Drugs Change the Brain*. The Netherlands: Harwood Academic Publishers, 1999 pp. lcII and 27.
7. "Nicotine Releases Chemicals in the Brian/The Addiction Process." Texas Medical Association, p. 2. http://www.texmed.org/cme/phn/ntd/process.asp.
8. "Smoking and Depression," Harvard Mental Health Letter, August 2002, p. 6.
9. Alan Leshner, "Addiction Research Can Provide Scientific Solutions to the Problem of Cigarette Smoking," NIDA Notes, Vol. 13, Number 3, 1998, p. 1.
10. "Nicotine Addiction," NIDA Research Report Series, 1998, pp. 2–3.
11. Neil Swan, "Like Other Drugs of Abuse, Nicotine Disrupts the Brain's Pleasure Circuit," NIDA Notes, Volume 13, Number 3, 1998, p. 1.
12. Kristine Napier, *Cigarettes: What the Warning Label Doesn't Tell You*, New York: American Council on Smoking and Health, 1996, p. xiv.
13. "Not Just Blowing Smoke," *Newsweek*, July 22, 2002, p. 8.
14. K.H. Ginzel, "What's in a Cigarette?" http://www.acsh.org/publications/priorities/0102/nicotine.html.

Chapter Three

1. "Questions and Answers About Cigar Smoking and Cancer," National Cancer Institute, *Med News*, November 6, 2002.
2. "Spit Tobacco: Just the Facts," Tobacco Control Research Branch, National Cancer Institute, Bethesda, MD, 2000.
3. "Children in India Becoming Addicted to Smokeless Tobacco," http://www.jointogether.org/sa/news/summaries/print/ 0,1856,553452,00.html.
4. Aaron Levin, "Flavored Asian cigarettes are even more deadly than regular ones." *Medical News Today,* May 4, 2004, http://www.medicalnewstoday.com/printerfriendlynews.php?newid_7931.
5. "Indonesian Kreteks High in Tar, Nicotine" www.jointogether.org, March 18, 2003.
6. John Leland, "When Smoke Gets in Your Pies," *The New York Times*, March 26, 2003.
7. "Activists Want Candy Cigarettes Stubbed Out," http://www.jointogether.org/sa/news/summaries/print/0,1856,562979,00.html.

Chapter Four

1. Avram Goldstein. *Addiction: From Biology to Drug Policy*. New York: Oxford University Press, 2001, p.119.
2. Kristine Napier, *Cigarettes: What the Warning Label Doesn't Tell You*. New York: American Council on Smoking and Health, 1996, p. 26.
3. Avram Goldstein, p. 126.
4. Report of the Surgeon General, "Preventing Tobacco Use Among Young People," Atlanta, GA: Centers for Disease Control and Prevention, 1994, p. 17.
5. "Many People with Asthma Still Smoke," http://www.join together.org/sa/news/summaries/print/0,1856,563292,00.html.
6. "The Health Consequences of Smoking," http://www1.worldbank/ tobacco/book/html/chapter 2.htm.
7. Kristine Napier, p. xiii.
8. Dr. C. Everett Koop review of *Cigarettes: What the Warning Label Doesn't Tell You*, New York: American Council of Science and Health, 1996, back cover.
9. "Opinion Interview" of Richard Peto, *The New Scientist*, September 2001, pp. 46–47.
10. Avram Goldstein, p.125.
11. Kristine Napier, p. 27.
12. Kristine Napier, pp. 27–30.
13. Kristine Napier, p. 26.
14. "Surgeon General Carmona Rejects Claims Smokeless Tobacco is a Safer Alternative to Cigarettes," http://www.tobaccofreekids .org/Script /DisplayPressrelease.php3?D.
15. Kristine Napier, "Alcohol and Tobacco: A Deadly Duo," http://www.acsh.org/publications/priorities/0102/alcohol.html.
16. Clare Wilson, "If You Can't Kick the Habit, Filter It," *The New Scientist*, June 28, 2003, p. 6.
17. "American Cancer Society Calls for Removal of Eclipse Cigarette from Marketplace," http://www.charitywire.com/00-02379.htm.
18. Special Report, Campaign for Tobacco Free Kids, January 4, 2001, http://www.tobaccofreekids.org/report/eclipse.
19. "USA Philip Morris to Help Map Cigarette Gene," http://www.tobaccoasia.com/news.asp?id=557.
20. "Breathing Easy," *U.S. News and World Report*, June 23, 2003, p. 44.
21. Kristine Napier, *Cigarettes: What the Warning Label Doesn't Tell You*, p.172.

Chapter Five

1. Jack W. Hill, "Clearing the Air," *Arkansas Democrat-Gazette*, January 6, 2003.
2. Centers for Disease Control and Prevention, "Second Hand Smoke," National Center for Chronic Disease Prevention, TIPS Fact Sheet, February 2004

3. Ibid.

4. Americans for Non-smokers' Rights, "Protecting Nonsmokers from Secondhand Smoke," January 8, 2003.

5. Elissa Gootman, "With Shrugs and Resignation, Smokers Watch a Final Haven Close." *The New York Times*, March 31, 2003.

6. Anahad O'Connor, "States Fail to Meet No-Smoking Goals for Women," *The New York Times*, September 30, 2003.

7. "Secondhand Smoke Ads Feature Smoking Babies," http://www.join together.org/sa/news/summaries/print/0,1856,5647.

8. Julie Rawe, "Smoke Signals," *Time* Bonus Section, November 2003.

9. "Smoking Health Hazards," http://pbskids.org/itsmylife/body/smoking /print_article2.html.

10. Alfred Morabia and others, "Involuntary Smoking Causes Breast Cancer Too." *American Journal of Epidemiology*, Vol. 148, pp. 1195–1205, December 1998.

11. Second National Report on Human Exposure to Environmental Chemicals, "Cotinine Fact Sheet." Atlanta, Georgia: Centers for Disease Control and Prevention, 2002.

12. Prabhat Jha, *Curbing the Epidemic*, Washington, D.C.: The World Bank, 1999, p. 4.

13. "Second Hand Smoke Kills," http://www.nyc.gov/html /doh/pdf/smoke /shsmoke2.pdf.

14. "WHO Unanimously OKs Tobacco Treaty," http://www.join together.org/sa/news/summaries/print/0,1856,563380,00.html.

Chapter Six

1. "Buying Influence, Selling Death" www.tobaccofreekids.org/reports /contributions.

2. "Big Tobacco is Messing With You," http://www.smokingstopshere.com /BigTobacco/youth.cfm.

3. Ibid.

4. Tara Parker-Pope, *Cigarettes: Anatomy of an Industry from Seed to Smoke*, New York: The New Press, 2001, p. 81.

5. Julep Cigarettes, http://www.chickenhead.com/truth/julep2_40 .html- truthinAdvertising.

6. Stuart Elliot, "Advertising: Joe Camel, A Giant in Tobacco Marketing, Is Dead at 23." *The New York Times*, July 11, 1977.

7. Teenz 247, http://www.teenz247.com.

8. Eric Lindbolm, "The Impact of Smoking in the Movies on Youth Smoking Levels," www.tobaccofreekids.org /research/factsheets/pdf/0216.pdf.

9. "Smoke Free Movies Go Deeper," http://www.smokefreemovies.ucsf.edu /godeeper/Landmark_study.html.

10. C. Meckemson and S.A. Glantz, "How the Tobacco Industry Built Its Relationship with Hollywood," Tobacco Control, 2002, www.tobaccocon- trol.com.

11. "Puffing Up a Storm," http://www.time.com/time/magazine/article/sub- scriber /0,10987,11.

12. "Scene Smoking: Cigarettes, Cinema and the Myth of Cool," http://www.cdc .gov/tobacco/celebrities/scenesmoking.htm.
13. "Thumbs Up! Thumbs Down! Hollywood," http://www.saclung .org/thumbs.
14. "Youth Tobacco Use and Exposure Is a Global Problem," CDC Press Release, August 28, 2002.
15. "How Do You Sell Death . . ." http://tobaccofreekids.org/campagn/global /FCTCreport2.pdf.
16. "New FTC Report Shows Tobacco Marketing Increased Nearly 67 Percent in Three Years After Settlement," http://www.tobaccofreekids .org/Script/DisplayPressRelease.php3?Display=656.
17. "About BADvertising Institute," www.badvertising.org.

Chapter Seven

1. Gene Borio, "Tobacco Timeline," http://www.tobacco.org/History/Tobacco _History.html.
2. Thomas E. Addison, M.D., "A Chronology of Tobacco in the Civilized World," p. 1, http://www.mindfully.org/Industry/ Tobacco-Chronology Jul98.htm.
3. "Highlights of Tobacco History," Coalition for a Tobacco Free Pennsylvania, Harrisburg: Pennsylvania Department of Health, 1998, p. 1.
4. Laurence Pringle, *Smoking: A Risky Business*. New York: Morrow, 1996, p.14.
5. CBS News-In depth: "Smoking Up a Storm," http://cbc.ca/news/indepth /smoking.
6. Addison.
7. Tobacco and Culture of the 17th and 18th Century America and Europe, http://www.adjunctcollege.com/nicotine6-ns4.html.
8. Addison.
9. Global Initiatives, http://www.tobaccofreekids.org/campaign/ global.
10. Personal correspondence, World Health Organization, October 13, 2004.
11. Cigarette Consumption Chart, Tobacco Free Initiative, http://tobacco .who.int/page.cfm?sid=84.
12. World Bank, "Measures to Reduce the Demand for Tobacco," p. 6, http://www1.worldbank.org/tobacco/book/html/chapter4.htm.
13. "World's Biggest Smoking Market," Tobacco Online, English edition, http://www.tobaccochina.com /english/news.asp?id=3886.
14. Tara Parker-Pope, *Cigarettes: Anatomy of an Industry From Seed to Smoke*, New York: The New Press, 2001, p. 50.
15. "Smoking Will Kill One Third of Young Chinese Men," http://www.hcc .hawaii.edu/~pine/Phil110/chinasmoking.html
16. Marc Lacey, "No-Smoking Signs Spread Slowly Across Africa," *New York Times*, February 2, 2003.
17. "Tobacco Habit Targets Women," http://www.twnside.org.sg/title/ habit.htm.
18. "Illicit Tobacco Trade Contributes to Global Disease Burden," http://www.who.int/mediacentre/releases /who62/en/print.html.
19. David Moyer, 'The Tobacco Reference Guide," http://www.globalink.org /tobacco/trg/Chapter2/Chap2_Toba_UsePage24.html.
20. Ibid.

Chapter Eight

1. David Kessler, *A Question of Intent*. New York: Public Affairs, 2001, p. 198.
2. W. Koch and K. Johnson K, "Government: Cover-up Lasted 45 Years," *USA Today*, September 23, 1999.
3. L. Bergman O. Zill, "Inside the Tobacco Deal," Frontline Online, www.pbs.org/wgbh/pages/frontline/shows/settlement/case.
4. Ibid.
5. L. Bergman, O. Zill. Loc.cit.
6. David Kessler, Op. cit. p.186.
7. W. Koch, K. Johnson. Loc. cit.
8. Ron Scherer, "New Front in the Tobacco Wars: Light Cigarettes," *Christian Science Monitor*, April 15, 2003.
9. "Philip Morris Loses Big in Illinois Lawsuit," www.jointogether.org/summaries/reader/0,1854,562354,00.htm March 25, 2003.
10. "Tobacco Settlement Is a Done Deal," *USA Today*, www.usatoday.com/news/smoke/279.htm.
11. R. Wolf, M. Kasindorf, "Tobacco Money to Aid Local Problems," *USA Today*, November 22, 1999.
12. National Conference of State Legislatures, "Health Care, Smoking Prevention Benefit from Tobacco Settlement Money," October 9, 2003, http://www.ncsl.org/programs/press/2003/ pr031009.htm.
13. Campaign for Tobacco Free Kids. Special Reports: State Tobacco Settlement. www.tobaccofreekids.org/reports/settlements. January 2003.
14. Ibid.
15. E. A. Smith, R. E. Malone, "Altria Means Tobacco: Philip Morris's Identity Crisis." Am J Public Health 2003; 93:553-556.
16. "New Study in the American Journal of Public Health Shows Philip Morris's Anti-smoking Ads Make Kids More Likely to Smoke," http://www.americanlegacyfoundation.org/section .asp?Page=41&id_63.
17. David Kessler, Op.cit. p. 388.

Chapter Nine

1. Shelly Fisher Fishkin, *Lighting Out for the Territory: Reflections on Mark Twain and the American Culture*. New York: Oxford University Press. 1996, pp. 133–137.
2. J. R. DiFranza and others, "Development of Symptoms of Tobacco Dependence in Youth" Tobacco Control 2002, 11:228–235.
3. Susan Brink, "No Light Smoking," *U.S. News and World Report*, June 17, 2002.
4. "Less Smoking but Same Number of Smokers," Washington, D.C.: *ASH Smoking and Health Review*, March–April 2003, p. 2.
5. Kirk Douglas, "My First Cigarette and My Last," *The New York Times*, May 16, 2003.
6. Michael Cummings and others: "You Can Set Yourself Free," Bethesda, MD, American Cancer Society, 2001.
7. Jayne Iafrate, "A Minute with Matt Strekel," *Wheaton Quarterly*, Spring 2003, p. 7.

8. "Quit Lines Effective in Helping Smokers," http://www.jointogether.org /sa/news/summaries/print/0,1856,554634,00.html.

9. "Internet Stop Smoking Programs Effective," http://www.jointogether.org /sa/news/summaries/print/0,1856,563010,00html.

10. "Study Tests Smoking Vaccine," http://www.jointogether.org/sa/news /summaries/print/0,1856,556105,00.html.

11. "Pfizer Unveils Anti-Smoking Drug," http://www.no-smoking.org/june03 /06-18-03-6.html.

Index